THE CHINESE MODEL

THE CHINESE MOON.

THE
Chinese Model

A POLITICAL, ECONOMIC AND SOCIAL SURVEY

EDITED BY

WERNER KLATT

Published under the auspices of
THE INSTITUTE OF MODERN ASIAN STUDIES
University of Hong Kong

HONG KONG UNIVERSITY PRESS

THE OXFORD UNIVERSITY PRESS, AMEN HOUSE, LONDON E.C.4
AND 417 FIFTH AVENUE, NEW YORK 16, ARE THE EXCLUSIVE
AGENTS FOR ALL COUNTRIES OF EUROPE, NORTH AMERICA,
AUSTRALIA AND NEW ZEALAND.

Printed in Hong Kong by
CATHAY PRESS
31 Wong Chuk Hang Road at Aberdeen

PREFACE

E. STUART KIRBY

This book makes a special and original contribution to the study of one of the most important issues of our age—the nature of the world-wide challenge and appeal of communism, and the direction which it may take henceforward. The outcome of the struggles and confrontations referred to in these pages might be decisive for the whole future of the world.

The practical and political basis of world communism was greatly widened and strengthened in the aftermath of the Second World War: on the one hand by the emergence of the Soviet Union as a victorious nation, and its subsequent development as one of the dominant powers; and on the other hand by the addition of a second gigantic communist country, China.

Both the U.S.S.R. and the People's Republic of China are formally committed *à l'outrance* to a world revolution. Judgments differ regarding how far, in practice and under testing circumstances, they are ready and able to sustain or implement that commitment; but none can doubt that it is a major, pressing and absolute aim of both China and Russia to spread communism over the rest of the world.

Both use for that purpose—in duality and in combination—some measure of pressure and some measure of persuasion (in varying recipes, according to time, place and circumstance). In respect of both Russia and China, the whole world is by now widely familiar with the pressures in question—military, political, commercial and other. Turning to the measures of persuasion, what is involved is clearly to achieve acceptance by the rest of the world of Russia and China as *models of progress* in all relevant respects.

The world is much more familiar with the attempts of Russia to gain acceptance in this way as a model than with those of China. It is with the ambitions of China, on this plane, that the following pages deal. The writers are selected experts, each taking up one aspect here especially; and the symposium closes with a summing-up by an eminent observer.

I should note at once that the attempt of China to secure acceptance internationally as a successful model to be emulated and imitated is very far from being a modest or limited one. Chinese endeavours in this respect seem to be largely unknown in Far Western countries, and their impact underestimated.

The Chinese propaganda has not, of course, been at work for so long a period as has the Russian. But it now appears to be as widespread, as studied, and as well supported with financial and personnel resources, as the Russian. This is not the place for a detailed description or analysis. Suffice it to say that the following aspects are well known and directly observable in Asia, Africa and Latin America, i.e. the underdeveloped areas, the Dark Crescent or Proletarian Hemisphere, it might be called, to which China naturally appeals mainly and primarily—though by no means neglecting the remaining areas, the white minority of the world.

Thousands of delegations, writers, artists, performers, students, and all kinds of people, usually in groups but sometimes as individuals, have travelled to and from China. The Chinese radio programmes are extensive, megavocal, and polyglot. A very large diffusion of films, printed matter, etc. is also of course in question. Hundreds of magazines, journals or newspapers are maintained, controlled or influenced by Mainland China. No propaganda means is neglected, down to postage stamps and pen-pals. All this is on a world-wide scale, though with special reference to the underdeveloped regions, and most specifically to Asia, where there is the closer image of China as an Asian power, and the Chinese as fellow Asian people.

At this writing, the disagreement between the Russian and Chinese Communist Parties stands fully revealed, in public clashes and affronts, and has even been documented in wordy exchanges of propaganda between the Parties themselves for all to see and know. The Chinese communists continue, in this confrontation, in the absolutely unyielding stand which they have taken, while the Russian communists are equally set to extend and intensify the debate, very widely and flexibly.

Both sides are determined that this is a crucial issue for the whole future of communism in the world, and are deeply committed to resolving it as soon as possible, and resolving it in terms of a dogmatic decision between two actual alternative paths to the World Revolution—a matter on which neither is willing or able to contemplate any compromise, except on a very temporary, partial or local plane.

With true Leninist firmness, both sides postulate that there is no middle way, that it is essentially a question—to mix the vocabularies of Lenin and Khrushchev—of 'who will bury whom', a crux to be resolved as quickly and unequivocally as possible. The disputants have exchanged what are, from the communist point of view, unforgivable insults such as the Chinese accusing the Russians of treachery, and the Russians accusing the Chinese of racialism and ultranationalism, over and above any questions of heresy.

A greater breach seems inevitable in the international communist movement, of a kind and intensity so far paralleled only by the cleavage between Stalin and Trotsky in the last generation, and equally deep, but now on a wider stage, and with much more disastrous potentialities for the future prospects of communism, and for world peace in general. The chosen arena, the prime and decisive point of dispute, is whether Peking or Moscow should lead and control the proletariat, and particularly the underdeveloped (developing or emerging) new nations of Asia, Africa and Latin America, and their peoples; and whether the Peking model or the Moscow model should be, for those nations and peoples in particular, the pattern and the example to be followed.

A full and expert study of China's claims to be THE MODEL, China's efforts to press these claims on the peoples of the underdeveloped regions in particular, and the latters' receptivity to them, is thus a most necessary and useful undertaking at this juncture.

In this dispute then, both contestants will strive all the harder to win friends and influence people, chiefly or rather essentially by establishing Russia or China, respectively, as the 'progressive' model. Russia is now the *arrivée*, the mature and experienced veteran, technologically and industrially advanced—well on, in a current economic formulation, into the drive to maturity, higher levels of consumption and so forth—evincing a wholesome caution about nuclear destruction, calling for coexistence, and professing considerable confidence in her power to win under conditions of peaceful competition.

China poses as the *arriviste*—the vigorous, rising, challenging, impatient, clear-headed, youthful champion. Seeing no need to parley with old fogeys and only illusion or danger in playing games under their rules, Communist China appeals especially to other youthful nations, or to regenerated old nations, now finding themselves in the prior stage of the take-off. The latter nations are those of the underdeveloped areas which, in basic Maoist doctrine, should encircle and overcome the urban areas, the industrially developed countries.

This book is an attempt to study the character, strength and perceptives of Communist China's bid for acceptance as the model which other countries should follow.

CONTENTS

CONTENTS

INTRODUCTION

WERNER KLATT

While all development circles are vicious, some are more vicious than others.

A. O. Hirschman, *The Strategy of Economic Development* (1959)

The centre of the world no longer lies in Europe. The Second World War has seen to that. New centres of power have emerged. The United States and the Soviet Union both have their attractions but neither always satisfies those searching for the key to development in the social, economic and political spheres. As long as there are two giants, the search will continue for a third way. Where can it be found?

Since the end of the last war, some fifty countries have gained their independence from foreign tutelage. This process began with Britain's loss of Singapore to Japan in 1942; it was accelerated when, after the war, Britain prudently decided to give up what could no longer be held. This process gathered momentum, and as a result few territories in the world remain under European metropolitan rule.

Only three remain in Asia—Hong Kong under Great Britain, and Macao and Timor under Portugal. Elsewhere in Asia large areas are under communist colonial rule: the central Asian republics are governed from Moscow, and Tibet has come under the control of Peking. In Africa, north and south of the Sahara, between the beginning of 1960 and 1961, eighteen countries gained independence in as many months; others have done so since, and still others will be free soon. All of them are in search of a model for their own future.

If independence is the end of a troubled journey, often through prisons and across battlefields, it is also the beginning of a new road no less arduous and perilous. What lies ahead is often as painful and always as unknown as what now belongs to the past. The growth into nationhood is not easy. It is a process which deserves the utmost attention and demands the widest experience. Few would be so presumptuous as to claim to have a ready answer to give to those in search of one.

Historians have isolated a number of propensities, beliefs and sets of values which exercised favourable influences on the growth of modern industrial societies, but these do not necessarily provide the models for our age. To give only one example: a generation of suffragettes had to fight before a measure of equality with men was granted to women in Western Europe; in some cantons of Switzerland voting rights are still withheld from women even today. Against this, in Asia and Africa millions of women have received the right to vote before attaining anything like a state of equality with men in professional or any other respect. In these circumstances it would be dangerous to draw parallels where none exist.

Whereas in the West men hesitate to offer a ready answer, the leaders of communist countries claim to have found solutions that are applicable everywhere. They present their type of society as the image of the future and their historical experience as a pattern that can be followed blindly by any newly-emergent country. Thus at a conference organized under the auspices of the United Nations early in 1963, the Russian delegates claimed that the Soviet Union had eliminated economic, social and political backwardness in the 45 years since the Bolshevik Revolution. They recommend their historic experiences as the pattern to be followed by the emerging nations in Asia, Africa and Latin America.

The leaders of Communist China claim that they are even better qualified than the Russian leaders to provide the model for countries engaged in freeing themselves from what the Chinese leaders define as foreign colonial rule and indigenous bourgeois tutelage. A variant has thus been added to the ideological controversy between the Soviet Union and the United States, between the familiar versions of the communist and capitalist approach. The conflict within the Sino-Soviet bloc has brought to the world's attention yet another model, anti-capitalist as well as pro-industrial; revolutionary rather than 'revisionist'; militant and not in favour of 'peaceful coexistence' within a divided world.

A nation which succeeds in making a complete break with its traditions and which refuses to accept any of the models that served others in their industrial development is bound to stir the imagination yet at the same time to confuse the minds of intellectuals in search of an idol. In China, conditions are sufficiently similar to those in emergent countries elsewhere to create a sense of understanding and sympathy for what the Chinese model is thought to be. Affinities are often so close as to be startling. What could be more natural in these circumstances than to view with curiosity, if not with affection, the possibility of a Chinese lead?

The intellectuals of newly-emergent countries tend to see the fruits of nationhood, social welfare and economic growth, without knowing much about the journey which the advanced countries have travelled and which the developing countries in turn will have to make so as to get within reach of those fruits. They are often in dire need of a record of their own past; and they do not always appreciate fully the amount of pain caused by the processes which turned the frozen societies in Europe through the Renaissance, the Reformation and the Enlightenment into the open industrial communities whose products are desired by all. They sometimes fail to recognise that, more than anything else, the readiness to choose and to decide is a precondition of change.

A full understanding of frozen societies is essential for making the right choice. The marks of a frozen society are farming as the chief form of economic activity and the village as the chief form of community. Within the village the expanded family is usually the focus of all that is done; its way of life is circumscribed by the watchful eyes of the village elders who recognize no privacy, without which no genuine political life develops. The village is often dominated by men who own most of the land, money and processing facilities, and who frequently spend as income what should be husbanded as capital. Apart from the cultivators, a surprisingly large number of people are employed in the villages outside agriculture but are held to its rhythm of life. Unless they conform, they become outcasts.

In these conditions opportunities are strictly limited; so are social and economic mobility. Change means disturbance of the existing pattern; it is thus suspect. Revelation rather than reason governs the relations between men and deity, and poverty is often considered meritorious. Insofar as towns exist they give the appearance of villages that have burst their seams. Even here human relations are often defined by custom rather than by economic reality.

Development only begins when traditional ties give way to economic relations. In Europe, religious beliefs were brought into line with secular interests before modern development started. Without the rationalization of the theological concepts and the secularization of political thought high rates of economic growth and modern forms of government might not have materialized. The European experience is worth studying also in other respects. As the large-scale ownership of land by a small minority often leads to abuses, the land question makes for discontent and demand for change. The contrast between growing needs and outmoded customs is felt acutely when commerce and industry expand and a money market takes the place of the subsistence economy. These facets of a developing society call for a sense of personal and public responsibility, of individual initiative and readiness to make decisions, which frozen societies can do without.

Developing countries, which are not yet in reach of this degree of advance are marked by the clash between traditional static conditions and the dynamism of advanced societies. The clash occurs frequently in the era of colonial rule; hence the violence with which the memory of the former metropolitan power is extinguished when independence is finally achieved. The dislocation of set values caused by foreign interference leads to a love-hate relation which does nothing to facilitate normal processes of political, economic and social development. The end products of Western society are desired, but the steps which led to the unique phenomena of this society are not recognized for what they are: a *conditio sine qua non*.

Lacking that spiritual process which developed in Western Europe at the end of the Middle Ages, the leaders of developing countries try short-cuts that may give them the fruits of development without the price which the Western society had to pay for its own development. Political solutions are thus often sought as substitutes for processes of economic and social growth. Political leadership and government, designed to cope with development tasks, take diverse forms ranging from the democratic experiment of India to the autocracies, military dictatorships and one-party régimes found in some parts of the Middle and Far East, Africa and Latin America. While their ideological concepts are fed by the springs of nationalism and anti-colonialism, they usually reject as unsuited to their conditions the doctrines which set communist régimes apart. In the choice between political freedom and economic development communist régimes have been alone in sacrificing entirely individual freedom to economic growth.

The Chinese model must be viewed in this context. The highly intelligent Chinese, tied to the soil, enduring famine and internal strife for three millennia, have moved with breathtaking speed from a frozen society to a nation in conflict with an outside dynamic world. Growing ever more ready for the release of a passion expressed by Sun Yat-sen before the First World War (1914–1918), the Chinese nation finally came under a leadership which put dogma above pragmatism. China thus became the second great country in the world whose leaders sacrificed political freedom for rapid economic and social change.

The views of sinologists and sovietologists trying to interpret current Chinese events have ranged from those considering the present state as the fulfilment of Chinese tradition to those seeing in it but a variant of the Soviet experiment. Anybody familiar with the teaching of both Confucius and Marx will discern the influences of both in the disciple now standing on his own feet. Patterned on the Soviet model, the concept of Marxism-Leninism has been modified by Mao and his Party to fit the specific conditions of China and the Chinese. Thus Chinese communism must be seen within the setting of China itself.

In China, as in other underdeveloped countries with a pre-industrial subsistence economy, there has always been much malnutrition, disease and rural underemployment; low labour mobility and small chances of non-farm employment. Urban unemployment has always been widespread, while farm tenancy and land fragmentation have caused low personal and national incomes, exorbitant land rents and interest rates, great indebtedness and little inclination to save and invest.

To understand what happened on the Chinese mainland when the rest of Asia, like Europe, was preoccupied with reconstruction after the most devastating of wars, some essential features must be borne in mind. First of all, her traditional society and a static economy had been challenged by commercial and other forces whose loyalties lay outside China and whose values were those of the Western world of the twentieth century. Confronted with forces never encountered before, the Chinese élite—the educated, landowning and ruling classes who in the past had governed poverty stricken, illiterate and powerless masses—proved helpless in face of such a mighty challenge. People were no longer prepared to accept set values without questioning, authority ceased to be sacrosanct and family loyalties lost their *raison d'être*. Missionary and commercial activities were bound to do their disruptive work whilst opening the way to modernity.

Secondly, there grew among those who had been dislodged in the course of the conflict, a group with a passionate desire to learn for the sake not of copying the faith and the way of life of the Western intruder—as had happened in the early stages of the Japanese industrial revolution—but of replacing them by a revolutionary creed which rested on both a nationalist and a socialist vow. Oppressive government and bureaucratic infringement had occurred more than once in the long history of China, and so had their corollaries, the secret societies and revolutionary organizations resorting to violence in preference to reform. The middle layer of society, which might have had a moderating influence in a process of deliberate change, was absent. Rulers and ruled were thus bound to come into conflict with ever increasing frequency.

Had it not been for the Japanese invasion, Western aid and know-how might have helped to complete a process of transition by reform which was well under way. As it was, the foreign aggressor provided the revolutionary conspiracy with the golden opportunity of identifying itself with the national goals of self-preservation and liberation. In this situation a return to the *status quo ante* would have been an anachronism. Thus China's destiny was decided by a determined group of professional revolutionaries, trained in the concept of historical materialism, determined to throw overboard the dead weight of tradition and ready to sacrifice all for the future of China and of communist world domination.

Revolutions tend to be all-inclusive in their aims, and in assessing them when and where they occur, we must beware of pre-judging them, taking an unsympathetic stand for fear of encouraging totalitarian terror in areas of pastoral peace. There are, however, elements that distinguish communist revolutions from all others in our time. To cite but one example: of the three overriding political considerations that determine communist economic policy, only capital expropriation and industrialization of the heavy type can be found elsewhere; but only under communist rule have village communities been forced to give up their land gained in the course of the revolution, in the name of 'socialist' collectivization. This concept flies in the face of all historical precedent and has thus proved unworkable in country after country, where communist minorities rule over non-communist majorities. Yet, no communist leadership has found it possible to do without collectivization, while non-communist upheavals have steered clear of this dangerous reef.

Communist rule in China did have at times certain features of moderation and gradualism. In fact, in the early years after the revolution they were so pronounced that some commentators tended to see in Mao Tse-tung the agrarian reformer rather than the communist revolutionary. The fallacy of this interpretation requires no further argument. The object of the operation was the gradual concentration of power in the hands of a monolithic party machine after the systematic elimination of all areas of dispersed power and of all spheres of alternative loyalty. This development was accompanied by the most effective form of human engineering ever known; and the most complete subordination of all governmental, military and economic organs under the control of the Communist Party was achieved.

The most terrifying features of this process, applied much faster and more effectively than in the fifteen years after the Bolshevik Revolution of 1917, were the various 'anti' campaigns directed against the remnants of the *ancien régime*, the so-called counter-revolutionaries and other sceptics and opponents of the new rulers. These campaigns created an atmosphere of fear on a scale which the modern world has probably never seen before, and against which the economic achievements of the régime, however impressive, cannot but pale.

Even the record of economic progress is not without blemish. The period of reconstruction after 1949 was followed by a 5-year plan that laid the foundations of a material basis, without which industrialization would have been impossible. When the infrastructure of the economy was put to a severe test during the second 5-year plan, it was found wanting in many respects. The teeming masses of men and women of rural China were no substitute for Soviet equipment and know-how, cut off when the clash of interests between the two communist giants could no longer be avoided. Within a year the experiment of the communes which were to simultaneously solve urban and rural tasks came to naught. The Great Leap Forward overreached itself and ended in retrenchment if not retreat.

Specialists in the yet unexplored art of national development have produced various interesting theories of growth. Some see orderly balanced progress as the target to be aimed at; whilst others stress the challenge which lies in unbalanced, disorderly processes. Both schools have contributed towards isolating the phenomena of growth, but one should not sidetrack the issue by posing the wrong questions. All processes of growth represent a break with the *status quo* and they are thus bound to move by fits and starts and therefore to be painful. However, physicians, educators, economic planners, social engineers and political reformers can help to alleviate the pains of growth.

However much the Chinese leaders may have achieved otherwise, in this particular respect they have rarely tried their hands. They do not comfort; they do not weigh the cost, in terms of money—let alone of human happiness—of their experiment. Here then lies a lesson to be studied by the leaders of developing countries before they decide whether to apply the Chinese pattern in the social, economic and political spheres of their own countries or whether to look, with a critical but open mind, at the patterns of development that have led to a more balanced process of growth.

Part I

Breaking with the Past:
A Sociological Survey

CHAPTER ONE

CHANGE OF SOCIAL VALUES

VICTOR FUNNELL

The aim of all our effort is the building of a new society and new nation of the Chinese people. In such a new society and new nation, there will be not only a new political organization and new economy, but a new culture as well.

MAO TSE-TUNG (1940)[1]

New society, new nation, new culture—this, no less, is the ambitious goal of China's rulers today. Controllers of the destiny of the most populous nation on earth, they have the power and the will to attempt an unprecedented process of human engineering. Although history has many examples of political oppression, physical compulsion, economic slavery, and doctrinal imposition, this is the first time that a régime has sought, consciously, to harness the very thoughts of the population, to change men's minds and their natural reflexes on a mass scale, and introduce a line of thinking approved by the authorities. To accomplish this colossal task the ground first needs careful preparation. The appeal is to patriotism, to the desire to achieve world-power status, to increased production in every field, to the sense of community, and the goal of national unity. Any individual, any institution, that might seem to provide a rival centre of attraction, economic, political, or ideological, must be ruthlessly uprooted. Such an obstacle existed—and judging from current evidence—still exists in the steady survival of that hardy institution, the Chinese family. To change society in the way the communists intend, it must be divested of all significance. The individual in society must be deprived of all traditional props to his way of life, isolated, so that he had better seek identity with the collective will, as represented by the Party, and merge his own consciousness in that of 'socialism'.

First destroy, then build. With the setting up of the People's Republic of China in 1949, the attack on the family began. In his guerilla days and at Yenan, Mao insisted that the first task was to build up base areas, and now the Communist Party in the 'loose sands' of Chinese society began to set up its bases. Techniques acquired during twenty years in the wilderness served to make a three-prong assault on the citadel of the family system through land reform, class struggle and ideological remoulding.

Land Reform: The Approach

The unsolved rural problems of the *ancien régime* gave the communists their great opportunity. Mao Tse-tung noted this during the Hunan uprising in 1927 and made it the subject of the lecture *On the New Democracy*, which he published at Yenan in 1940 during the war against Japan: 'It is the common knowledge of every primary schoolboy that 80 per cent of the Chinese population consists of peasants. Therefore the peasant question becomes the fundamental question of the Chinese revolution, and the force of the peasantry is the main force of the Chinese revolution'.[2] By land reform the communists would undermine the economic base of the existing social order.

'The new democratic republic will adopt certain necessary measures to confiscate the land of big landlords and distribute it among peasants without any, or with very little land, in order to realize Dr Sun's slogan, "The tiller should own his own land", and to liquidate the feudal relations in rural areas.'[3] 'Confiscation' implies 'millet plus rifles', to use Mao's own graphic phrase.[4] It was a bid for the support of the landless peasants in a common identity of purposes. By changing man's relation with man, it was thereby altering his relationship with the state.

In his land reform, Mao acknowledges his debt to Dr Sun Yat-sen, the founder of the Chinese Republic in 1911, and to Dr Sun's *Three People's Principles*, of nationalism, democracy and the people's livelihood (socialism). Nationalism meant unity and a strong unified government. Therefore the masses had to be awakened and brought into the governing process. To do this the government had to remedy poverty and level the gross inequalities, and took for slogan 'Land to the tiller' in their agrarian reform movement. In this both Dr Sun and Chairman Mao went against traditional concepts for they understood that the government must have greater direct contact with the people. But with communism the Party was to enter the people's homes. From the beginning, land reform and the class struggle went hand in hand.

Land Reform in Action

The communists proceeded at once on the basis of class. Everybody had to have his or her classification—landlords, rich peasants, middle peasants, poor peasants or hired labourers. Forms were sent to everybody and from the replies, a class label was assigned to each villager. From the complaints it was sometimes hard to know whether social origin or a revolutionary standpoint determined class. At times the standard of living seemed to give a clue. 'Even if old Wang hasn't so much land, he always manages to eat meat dumplings every full moon, and there's no saying how many times a month he eats wheat-flour noodles.'[5]

Following this classification came the 'Divide the Family' campaign: the whole village should 'struggle' against selected victims in 'speak bitterness' meetings. By such meetings the masses were brought immediately into the land-reform campaign and it could then be claimed it was a spontaneous demand of the people and not a policy officially inspired and imposed. The campaign was also planned as a social education of the people; the Party cadres put in weeks of preparation to ensure the success of each mass meeting.

The victims of 'struggle' could be divided into three categories. The 'third-class struggle objects' were accused of minor offences and were punished by being excluded from the Communist Peasant Union, which not only deprived them of political rights in local government, but also brought social ostracism, since the Union had become, with the ending of the old family ancestral ceremonies, the centre of the village social life.

The 'second-class struggle objects' were excluded not only from the Peasant Union, but also from the mutual-aid peasant groups. Their children could not attend school, a ruling dictated by the fact that in the past education and power had usually gone hand in hand. The 'first-class struggle objects' were the worst offenders, who not only suffered the disabilities of the other two 'objects', but were also obliged to wear a patch on their jackets inscribed with some such words as 'Landlord. First-class struggle object. Underminer of the democratic movement'.[6] This will remind readers of the Star of David compulsorily worn by all Jews during the Hitler régime in Nazi Germany—those that were not exterminated.

Such was China's land-reform procedure. The 'speak bitterness' often turned into a communal bloodlust. The unfortunate victim, kneeling in front of his accusers, might receive the communal death sentence, at the hands of villagers, neighbours, friends and even members of his own family. Mao Tse-tung himself has said approximately half-a-million people perished in this manner up to the beginning of 1957.[7] This happened presumably during the land reform, and subsequent collectivization.

By introducing categories of classes with which the peasants were previously unfamiliar, by extensive documentation and classification, by prolonged investigation and encouragement from Party cadres, by making the villagers themselves the instruments of mass campaigns and official policy (with the ultimate sanction of force), and finally by redistributing the land, the communists were able to advance towards their goal of building 'a new society and a new nation'.

The Measure of Change

To assess the measure of social change wrought by land reform it is necessary to look briefly at the old family system in the preceding decades. Often farms were entirely family enterprises, as were most units of production, such as a shop, a boat or a craft.[8] The head of the unit was naturally, therefore, the father, or in his absence or retirement, the eldest son. His would be the decision (not excluding, of course, family consultation), as to the way to employ resources and to direct labour. The land, the house and the tools were regarded as family property, and the deeds of possession were usually in the name of the family, and not of any one individual. Upon the death of the parents, the inheritance was divided among all the male heirs, with the eldest son getting a somewhat larger share for he was the celebrant responsible for the ancestor worship rites. The system rested on certain rules of sex and age. The constant subdivision of land accounted for the smallness of farms, and the scattering of plots belonging to the farm.

With few exceptions the family was related to the bigger unit, the clan, and played a role within it, if only to elect the clan's business manager or assistant. The elders of the clan were not elected but were eligible for office on reaching the age of 65, provided they were prepared, or able, to give a celebration feast to the clan—an undertaking that could be expensive when the clan was large. The functions of the clan, acting in its corporate role, were fairly widespread, and it could deal with matters too large for a family to handle by itself.

The clan thus functioned as a local government in the interests of its members. It also owned communal land, and with its proceeds were maintained the clan school and the ancestral halls. Not the least of the functions of the clan was the worship of ancestors. The ancestral hall, the repository of the very *lares et penates* of the clan, was the scene of sacrificial ceremonies, the observance of the rites, every spring and autumn. The tie of blood was strong. The clan could also act as an unofficial arbitrator, or court, in disputes affecting its members, and it could enforce social and moral order. As an entity, a unit of society, this whole close-meshed system of family and clan possessed great power, and any individual or family who stood outside it would be socially isolated, and might even find it hard to make his living.

Such a system was a challenge to the communists and fully explains the attempt to 'atomize' the individual through land reform. Clan land, of course, was not immune from the communist process of confiscation and redistribution, and this naturally affected those functions of the clan concerning ancestor worship and education. Moreover the internal structure of the family had been altered. Since land was redistributed regardless of sex or age, both young people and women were more favoured than under the traditional system. Women, under the regulations, could even take their land out of the family, for instance in case of divorce.[9] Another divisive factor was the introduction of class criteria in place of the old kinship relationship. Landlords and peasants might be from the same clan but kith and kin had been set at odds. 'The process of struggle had difficulty in getting started, especially when the case involved the young bringing charges against the old, but after the inhibition of kinship was broken down, the struggle became bitter.'[10]

Something else should be noted. Whereas, previously the collective identity had been with the clan, and the individual or family in their own interest had sought this identity, now the collective identity was with the Peasant Union and behind it the Communist Party, which only as individuals could they join and not in families. Yet, although the clan had been replaced a note of the clan spirit survived: 'When the village cadres did something wrong, older men named Li or Fu might be heard to mumble that most of the cadres were Wangs— though this point was not especially emphasized when things were going well'.[11]

All these radical changes, however, did not sufficiently eradicate the old ways, the old thoughts. In 1953 communist leaders were concerned at 'the growth of capitalist development on a free basis on the foundations of the small peasant economy'.[12] The movement of peasants into co-operatives then began. Peasant resistance in 1954 provoked social disorder, and an exodus from the countryside to the urban centres. 'The movement for co-operatives will not be a very peaceful one; it will be a deeply rooted and extensive class struggle.'[13] Once again the weapon of class struggle was used in the rural areas.

The development of the movement, and its later extension into the communes are too recent to require comment. Suffice it to say, that in the retreat from the communes since 1960, the family seems to have survived as a unit of work. There is also evidence that private ownership of property, houses and tools has survived or been restored.[14] The *Peking Review* referred quite frankly to the 'dual status of the peasant, as labourer and as private owner'.[15] Furthermore, there has been a modest restoration of land to the peasants for their private use—something like five per cent of the cultivable acreage.[16] Though this proves the tenacity of the Chinese family (to which the régime has had to make concessions), Chinese leaders have not given up their long-term goals. If the campaign against the family on the economic front has not been entirely successful, it is only a setback in the class struggle which continues.

The Barrage Continues

China's social fabric has been under open attack without respite; the totalitarian régime brings all its forces of propaganda and agitation to bear on the class struggle, to maintain the people's vigilance against 'reactionaries', to praise the heroes of communist virtues and to exhort all to build 'socialism'. This relentless flow of propaganda suggests that the Party has not succeeded in all that it had set out to do. *Red Flag*, the

Party's theoretical journal, in an editorial published in two successive issues in 1962, after claiming that more than ninety per cent of the population 'support socialism', admitted: 'Persons opposing socialism only account for a few per cent of the total population of our country. But it should not be considered that the more than ninety per cent of the people of different classes and various strata have spontaneously stepped onto the road of socialism, nor should we be convinced that the influence of the additional few per cent of the people will never expand in any circumstances'.[17] Assuming that the persons opposing socialism amount to about ten per cent of the population, this would give a rough figure of sixty million people. Nor can it be said, admitted the *Red Flag*, that the rest support socialism 'spontaneously'. This is a very honest statement.

The Marriage Law

If individuals were to be 'liberated' from the social claims of old affections and ties, the relationship between the members of a family had to be drastically changed and that of the women in particular. If land reform improved the economic status of women, the marriage law of May 1950 sought to alter their social position. Marriage henceforth was to be by mutual consent of the two parties, and not arranged by the parents. The age of consent was raised to 20 for males, and 18 for females. Husband and wife would be equal in status in the home, both could use their own family names, and there were provisions for divorce. This carried into effect Article 6 of the *Common Programme* adopted by the first session of the Chinese People's Political Consultative Conference, in September 1949: 'The People's Republic of China shall abolish the feudal system which holds women in bondage. Women shall enjoy equal rights with men in political, economic, cultural, educational and social life. Freedom of marriage for men and women shall be put into effect'.

This was done, as with so much in Communist China, in a mass campaign. ' . . . Every organization must co-operate. There is work to be done in schools, youth organizations, workers' unions and cultural organizations. The people must be brought together at public accusation meetings to expose those who have failed to live up to the standard of the new law. There must be huge mass trials. The marriage reform is to go hand in hand with land reform. The same technique is to be used for both.'[18]

There is no need to follow the usual development of this mass campaign in all its details. One result of the campaign should, however, be noted. At a meeting of cadres and students of Chahar province in May 1950, Teng Ying-ch'ao, vice-chairman of the All-China Democratic Women's Federation and wife of Premier Chou En-lai, asked and answered the rhetorical question: 'Will it not lead to reckless marriage and social disorder when we practise freedom of marriage, and grant divorce if either the husband or the wife insists upon it? It will not'.[19] Yet, the communists two years later gave the number of divorces as 186,000 in 1950, 409,000 in 1951, and 396,000 in the first six months of 1952, a steady and even spectacular increase.[20]

If the number of divorces increased, so did the number of suicides—over 10,000 in one region alone in the first six months of enforcement of the new law. Once again, the leadership had to call a tactical retreat. New instructions explicitly stated that the marriage law was 'different from land reform', 'no violence' was to be used, and that the purpose of the marriage law was not to break up marriages, but to bring peace. There were, of course, many instances of peasant resistance to the new law, and adherence to time-honoured practices. Even so, women did begin to emerge from their seclusion to attend meetings, to join Women's Associations, and even to take part in amateur theatricals.[21] They also became more and more prominent in everyday working life. The authorities were no longer remote from the people and now had a say in marital affairs. 'In order to contract a marriage, both the man and the woman shall register in person with the People's Government of the sub-district or village in which they reside. If the marriage is found to be in conformity with the provisions of this law, the local People's Government shall, without delay, issue marriage certificates.'[22]

The Past Swept Away

Thus the communists deeply penetrated the very homes of the people. They undid the ties that bound man to man, and man to the state, those paternal, benevolent relationships which had served in the past to harmonize conflicting interests; these bonds were many, but fundamentally they were three: the relationship of the emperor to his subjects, the husband to the wife and the father to the son.[23]

But the communists were not the first to initiate family reforms. The so-called 'family revolution' had been going on for two generations at least, although mainly confined to the upper and middle classes in the urban centres. Nor was it surprising that it should have been so. With greater facilities for physical and social mobility, how could the old relationships survive?

The cities were the centres of pre-revolutionary social changes and the 'seedbed' of ideas. This was true in particular of the universities. Mao Tse-tung himself, his mentor Li Ta-chao, and Ch'en Tu-hsiu, the first leader of the Chinese Communist Party, were all at Peking University, and the Party itself was founded in the city of Shanghai. And yet it was in the country-side that the Party found its soul and its present leader. It was at Yenan, in Shensi, that the Party doctrine and its practice received their full rehearsal. This experience continues to colour the attitude of China's present leaders towards the cities and the class struggle. It was a main influence in the 'five-anti' campaign in 1952.

Ostensibly a drive against bribery, tax evasion, fraud, theft of state property, and leakage of state economic secrets, this campaign was officially described as 'a counter-offensive to repel the ferocious attacks of the bourgeoisie', and their 'sugar-coated bullets'.[24] The cities of the plain, Sodom and Gomorrah, were centres of vice. Speaking in January 1952, Yeh Chieh-ying, secretary of the South China Bureau, and mayor of Canton, charged that, 'Some of our comrades . . . underwent a change of attitude towards corruption and waste after they came to the city; first abhorring it, they gradually became used to it, and finally loved it'.[25]

The appeal was made to the people to come forward as informers and denounce offenders. They were offered protection and their jobs were guaranteed. The struggle was carried into families and homes by means of mass meetings, cadres' visits to private homes, and the denunciation, over loudspeakers, of those who had not yet confessed.[26] Sons denounced fathers, wives their husbands, and employees were encouraged to denounce their employers by the hundreds and thousands.

All Things Made New

China's communists believe fanatically that what they are doing is morally and socially right, and that they hold the pass to an earthly paradise. 'Comrades! The Communist Party member should possess the greatest and noblest human virtues. At the same time he should adopt a strict and clear Party and proletarian standpoint (the Party and class spirit). Our moral stature is great precisely because it is proletarian and communist. This moral stature is not built on a foundation which is reactionary and protects the interests of a few individuals and exploiters, but on the progressive foundation of proletarian interests and the interests of the final liberation of mankind, of the salvation of the world from oppression, and the building of a happy, beautiful communist world.'[27]

Here is a ringing declaration of faith. There can, apparently, be no other road to man's salvation. 'To sit on the fence is impossible. . . . Not only in China but also in the world, without exception, one either leans to the side of imperialism or to the side of socialism. Neutrality is mere camouflage and a third road does not exist.'[28] 'Any action which is favourable to the proletariat is good and moral. The reverse is evil and immoral.'[29] Their new morality is 'the collective spirit, passionate love of labour, to be honest and frank, humility and prudence, patriotism and internationalism, and morality of the household, of marriage, and everyday life'.[30]

To proselytize the new faith, to instil the new principles in the hearts and minds of the people, the answer lies in a series of 'rectification' campaigns, indoctrination campaigns and self-criticism meetings. The *People's Daily*, on 5 January 1961, defined what this meant: 'The rectification movement, a common Marxist-Leninist ideological movement, is the principal method for correctly handling contradictions inside our Party. Its purpose is, by means of self-education and criticism and self-criticism, to clear up ideological matters, to improve understanding, and to distinguish between what is Marxist and what is not'.

Thus will the people's mind be transformed. Sins may be committed, but salvation is at hand. Party members live in a class society and non-proletarian thought causes them to commit errors. Some brought bourgeois thoughts into the Party with them; others entered only physically the Party organization, 'trusting in their own righteousness', but without ideological transformation. An article in the *Red Flag* of 23 January 1963 said: 'Educating and transforming Party members is part of the task, undertaken by the political Party of the proletariat, of transforming the old world'. Thus in Mao's phrase, it is possible 'to treat the illness to save the patient'. Penitence is followed by redemption, and not only for the 'chosen people', i.e. Party members, but for all others as well.

What is good for the Party is good for the nation and even mankind.

When the 10th Plenary Session of the Eighth Central Committee of the Chinese Communist Party, in September 1962, called for a strengthening of political education throughout China, a campaign of indoctrination spread out across the country, to army units, to the youth movement and schools, to labour unions, to peasants and to intellectuals. Its main themes were patriotism, internationalism, socialism, collectivism and the superiority of the collective economy. The classical texts are those of Marxism-Leninism and the works of Mao Tse-tung.

As the *China Youth Journal* expressed it, on 22 January 1963, 'When you come across new words, consult the dictionary; when you come across problems, consult the selected works of Mao Tse-tung'. The methods used are adapted to the audiences addressed. Perhaps the most famous campaigns of this nature took place in 1942 in Yenan, and in 1957 during the period of the Hundred Flowers. The 1957 campaign began as an apparent invitation to the critics of the régime to speak their minds on certain 'contradictions', such as those between city and country, the Party and public, and the main racial group and the minorities. But three months later a violent campaign was turned against those very critics.

'Struggle meetings' were held for days on end.[31] The critics, labelled as 'rightists', were made to confess. Accusation and abuse were hurled at them, until the desired object had been achieved, 'to destroy the prestige of the potential rebels, and the banners which could be raised against communism. This was what "ideological struggle" meant'.[32] Not long afterwards, the 'rightists' received their sentences. Some were sent to labour camps or farms, others were demoted or discharged, and all continued to bear the label of 'rightist'. Among them some were shot.

The Intellectuals

That the great majority of 'rightists' are to be found among the class of intellectuals is not surprising, for in its ideological struggle the régime has had the greatest difficulty with the intellectuals. They have naturally proved more resistant to remoulding. They are traditionally China's leading and ruling class, and just as much as the communists wish to win their allegiance, no less many intellectuals will not yield. 'Today, most of the intellectuals cannot catch up with the development of the great favourable situations inside and outside the country.' 'Not a few of them have not yet established the viewpoint of letting politics take command.' 'Some people were still sceptical about whether the Party could lead the work of scientific research in practical affairs.' 'A physics professor even said, "Yours is the proletarian world outlook, and mine is the bourgeois world outlook. So long as I abide by the constitution I am all right".' These quotations are taken from a report on meetings of intellectuals, published in the Peking *Kuang-ming Jih-pao* in January 1961;[33] they reveal the state of mind of the intellectuals.

But not all the intellectuals are opposed to the régime, though it should be remembered that the contact of Chinese intellectuals with communism has a long history. Two professors at Peking University, Ch'en Tu-hsiu and Li Ta-chao, founded the Chinese Communist Party in 1921. Peking University, in fact, was the institution at the heart of the whole reform movement which came to be known by the name of 'May the Fourth' [1919].

If the communists were able to attract a large measure of support from intellectuals in the course of their rise to power, it rests in part on their claim to be the heirs of the May Fourth movement; that the road to salvation for China lay in remedying her social ills; and that only the Communist Party had the will power and the strength to achieve it. But when in 1949, the communists came to power they perverted and traduced the ideals of China's social revolution. 'Totalitarianism in Asia as elsewhere is not a mere revival of things past but a new invention of modern times.'[34]

NOTES

[1] Mao Tse-tung, 'On The New Democracy' (1940), as found in *A Documentary History of Chinese Communism* by Brandt, Schwarz and Fairbank (Allen and Unwin, London 1952).

[2] *ibid.*

[3] *ibid.*

[4] Mao Tse-tung, in 'A talk with Anna Louise Strong', in his *Collected Works* (Foreign Languages Press, Peking 1961) Vol. 4: 101.

[5] I. and D. Crook, *Revolution in a Chinese Village—Ten Mile Inn* (Routledge & Kegan Paul, London 1959): 147.

[6] *ibid.*

[7] Mu Fu-sheng, *The Wilting of the Hundred Flowers* (Heinemann, London 1962), p. 128. Other estimates go as high as 14 million. See R. E. Walker, *China under Communism* (Allen and Unwin, London 1956): 219.

[8] Nanchang, near Canton, C. K. Yang, *A Chinese Village in Early Communist Transition* (Cambridge, Mass. 1959): 91 *et seq.*

[9] C. K. Yang, *op. cit.*, 179.

[10] *ibid.*

[11] I and D. Crook, *op. cit.*, 166

[12] Teng Tzu-hui, director of Rural Work Department, Central Committee of the Chinese Communist Party, July 1953: quoted by H. A. Steiner, *Chinese Communism in Action* (Univ. of California, 1963): chapter 11.

[13] Teng Tzu-hui, *Chung-kuo Ching-nien Pao* (1 April 1954): quoted by L. Trivière, 'Chinese agriculture and the Party', in *Saturn Review*, 2(i)(Jan.–Feb. 1956).

[14] U.R.S. (Union Research Service, Hong Kong), 28, No. 12 (10 August 1962).

[15] Kao Cheng-sheng, 'New-type urban-rural relations in China', in *Peking Review*, 29 March 1963.

[16] U.R.S. 28, No. 12 (August 1962).

[17] *Hung Chi*, in *Summary of World Broadcasts* (S.W.B.), 10 February 1962.

[18] Franz Michael, 'The role of law in traditional, nationalist, and Communist China', in *China Quarterly*, 9 (Jan.–Feb. 1962): 140.

[19] Teng Ying-ch'ao, *On the Marriage Law of the People's Republic of China*, (Foreign Languages Press, Peking 1950).

[20] Franz Michael, *op. cit.*, 141.

[21] C. K. Yang, *op. cit.*, 178.

[22] Marriage Law, Article 6.

[23] Fung Yu-lan, *Short History of Chinese Philosophy* (Macmillan Co., New York 1948).

[24] T. H. and W. C. Chen, 'Three-anti, Five-anti', in *Pacific Affairs*, 26(i) (March 1953).

[25] Yeh Chien-ying, member of Central Committee of the Party, secretary of the South China Bureau, and mayor of Canton: quoted by H. A. Steiner, *op. cit.*, chapter 10.

[26] T. H. and W. C. Chen, *op. cit.*

[27] Liu Shao-ch'i, 'On the training of a Communist Party member' (August 1939), in Brandt, Schwarz, and Fairbank, *op. cit.*

[28] Mao Tse-tung, 'On the People's Democratic Dictatorship' (July 1949), in Brandt, Schwarz and Fairbank, *op. cit.*

[29] Lo Kuo-chieh, *Kuang-ming Jih-pao* (14 December 1961), in U.R.S., 27, No. 10 (May 1962).

[30] *ibid.*

[31] Mu Fu-sheng, *op. cit.*, 169.

[32] *ibid*, 170.

[33] U.R.S., 23, No. 8 (28 April 1961).

[34] Brandt, Schwarz and Fairbank, *op. cit.*, 482.

CHAPTER TWO

THE COMMUNIST ATTITUDE TOWARDS RELIGION

JOSEPH R. LEVENSON

Introduction

As a Chinese, the Chinese communist never lets the West forget the Opium War*—a sinister name. As a communist, the Chinese communist never forgets a sinister metaphor—'opium of the masses': religion. In the last analysis there is nothing to say in its favour. Religion is idealistic and hence in his view anti-scientific; it is a slavery of the mind, a relic of outworn social systems, and will vanish when exploitation ends. But the last analysis is not so easy to reach. There are several steps before the last, before the simple anathema, and the Chinese past—not just the communist will—affects the Chinese communist's thinking on the problem of religion.

To begin with, the Chinese literati, whose temper was deeply conservative, were leaders in the old imperial society (*feudal* in the communist lexicon). And the literati by and large had never been happy about religion. Popular rebellions, which they hated, usually seemed to be fired with Taoist, Buddhist, Muslim, Christian or syncretic enthusiasm. From a Confucian point of view, religion could be a dangerous stimulant to the masses rather than an opiate. Therefore from a Chinese communist's point of view as well, its status is ambiguous.

---

* In 1839 Commissioner Lin Tse-hsü was sent by the Emperor to Canton to put an end to the opium trade. These orders he attempted to carry out by seizing and destroying 20,000 chests of the drug, owned by the foreigners, which led to the so-called Opium War of 1841–1842. While in office he dispatched a long letter to Queen Victoria, calling upon her to prohibit the export of opium from her dominions to China. See Arthur Waley's *The Opium War through Chinese Eyes*, London 1958.

The communists see themselves at a point of historical synthesis. They are true to the dialectic, and true to a modern Chinese need for an anti-traditional, yet still a Chinese history. 'Anti-feudal', they mean to relegate Confucian China firmly to the past—'anti-imperialist', they mean to repel that other foe of Confucian China, the West. Accordingly, a 'people's tradition' comes in for loving care. Non-literati and non-Western, it has obvious points in its favour. But pre-modern and pre-communist, it can hardly be taken as the last word, or what would the communists' occupation be? Hence, religion as a popular expression, non-literati, often anti-literati, wins a kind of indulgence; but it also awaits a final dismissal. That is what Mao implied in 1927, when he declared, 'Buddha was erected by the peasants'. This had a nice ambiguity. It was an argument for gradualism, for at least a passing respect for a 'people's religion'. And it was an argument, ultimately, for atheism.

Christianity: Between anti-Imperialism and anti-Confucianism

Christianity, as the latest comer, was historically the most foreign and least 'people's' of the religions in China. Its embroilment with imperial powers was easy to establish. Missionary on deck, opium in the hold—the metaphorical possibilities were too crudely obvious. And after the soporific, the explosives. The communists, projecting the idea of a creed discredited by cynical politics, simply touched up an old horrendous image: the gunboat, extracting quite worldly indemnification from China for having taken a bit of direct action against uninvited priests. And Christians were further damned as hypocrites, pious front-runners of imperialist aggressors, for their very charities in China. For these (so runs the charge), just in their seeming altruism, were sweetening the poison.

Where does that put the Chinese Christians in Communist China today? They are obliged, over and over again, to disclaim ties with the imperialist wreckers on the outside. There is an article on freedom of religion in the 1954 constitution, and Christian bodies still exist formally. Of course, the blood of martyrs has classic possibilities, and the régime does not choose to risk them. But more than that, tame Christians, left alive, serve the régime instead of threatening it. For what do these pathetically loyal national bodies achieve, this Chinese Catholic Patriotic Association, this Chinese Protestant Three Autonomies Patriotic Movement? Their very attempts to remove the foreign stigma, their protestations of anti-imperialism, only bear out the official idea that the church is naturally suspect, in a Christian-foreign, subversive-aggressive alliance. When Christians protest so ritually their innocence, it suits the communists better than official prosecution; the public will get the approved message from those who protest too much.

The communists hit Christianity not only in their 'anti-imperialist' but in their 'anti-feudal' character. That is, Christianity suffers directly for its association with the West, and also, less directly, for its *dissociation* from Confucianism. The communists choose science as their watchword—science, not as a cultural force from the West but as a universal solvent of the errors of the past. They are anti-Confucian in the name of science. And they are anti-Christian in the name of science, not just because Christianity, as a religion, must be under the ban of scientific socialism, but because they need a Western spiritual relic to match the pervasive, but now *passé*, Confucian spirit. If Christianity, too, can be dismissed as an anachronism in a scientific age, then one can wave goodbye to Confucian China without deserting China. When Christianity, rejectable, is taken as Western, science, so indispensable, can be taken as universal. 'Mediaeval' means Confucian China *and* Christian West; then 'modern' means a science-governed world. In a China that wants to industrialize, yet not pay tribute to the West, Christianity, posed against science, is ballast to throw away—to right the national balance when Confucianism, as the Chinese victim of science, has also been discarded.

General Popular Religion:
Between Mass Expression and Mass Deception

Because Christianity was foreign, it was doomed to be cast off as a 'feudal' sacrifice. It served as a parallel to native, outmoded Confucianism. But indigenous religions were affected otherwise by the fate of Confucianism, fate of the high culture (of the highly placed) brought low. On the whole, these religions belonged to the lowly placed and were traditionally disdained as culturally low. Therefore, anti-traditionalists had to revise the estimate. Confucianism, when challenged by the West of the 'imperialists', had to be defended, if only by a *tu quoque*, the spurning of Christianity. But Confucianism, cherished by the 'feudalists', had to be challenged at home. At least modest respect had to be paid to the creeds of those whom the 'feudalists' exploited.

The communists preferred historically identifiable creeds, which could be retired honourably to 'historical significance', praised for their past in the Marxist historical process, but properly beached upstream. Taoism and Buddhism, somewhat artificially abstracted from eclectic religious life, answered this description better than the congeries of popular cultic practices. These, having no known beginnings, looked intractably as though they might have no end, and communist patience became rather frayed. More as a matter of tactics than of friendly appreciation, communist political workers, during the war against Japan, were told to respect the religious beliefs of the popular secret societies. After their victory in the civil war, communist authorities were less benign. People like *yin-yang** experts and fortune-tellers and spirit-mediums were put down; after 1958 especially, the ancestor-cult was seriously discouraged. There was still some grain of acceptance for

---

* *Yin-yang* 陰陽. The two Chinese characters depict the shady or north, *yin* slopes of a hill and its sunny or south, *yang* slopes. This *yin-yang* concept of the dual nature latent in all things pervades the Chinese view of life and their everyday language, for nothing is so dark that it has not a sunny side, so cold that it has no warmth, so soft that it has no hardness, and so forth.

'religion of the masses'. But there was a rising note of menace against the 'use of religion by the reactionary class'.

Taoism: Between Superstition and Science

Religious Taoism, while certainly no smooth-working ecclesiastical machine, had more of a visible structure than the amorphous cults, and more of a line of history. Thus, there was something for the régime to see, to organize bureaucratically, and to historicize intellectually.

Earlier in the twentieth century, in Chinese radical circles, popular Taoism was usually written off as an excrescence of the old society. It was taken to be an incubus of ignorance, backward, anti-scientific mystagogy. And there was a tendency to see Taoism, socially, as a refuge for failures in 'feudal' society, an escapist corollary to exploitative Confucianism.

But communist victory over 'feudal' society (or 'semi-feudal, semi-colonial') brought the chance, and the need, to soften the tone. Once the grip of the leaders of the old society, at both its higher and lower levels, was broken, the passions of the struggle to break it might be allowed to cool, and old ideas be relativized to history. The very moribundity of Taoism made it acceptable for *historical* rehabilitation, now that its dead hand had been shaken off the present. Commentators on Taoism began to find in it not so much depressing quietism but rousing rebellious action, not just superstitious magic but the seeds, and some of the fruits, of science.

There was really something to work on here. The aim of classical, philosophical Taoism was mystic union with eternal Tao, the first principle of all things, eternal, impersonal, immanent in all. But popular Taoism, prominent since Han times, emphasized the physical, and one can see in it a set of physical parallels and parodies of the philosophical concepts. All sorts of diatetic, respiratory, and alchemical practices abounded.

The latter were most important for attracting modern sympathy. There had been a long search for ways to transform elements of matter, in hopes of finding an elixir of life. This included such efforts as to arrive at the *essence* of gold—that is, to separate its immanent *tao* from dross, so as to get a potable form of underlying reality. And there was another sort of alchemy, to the same end: the effort to produce 'life-preserving' substances like jade and cinnabar artificially, to release them from the inhibiting 'impurities' of their natural state. From here it was not far to secular goals like those of Western alchemy and proto-chemistry, such as efforts to make gold from baser metals. That is how the affinities of science in China came to be mainly popular-Taoist. It was quite consistent of Confucianism, looking with such fearful scorn on Taoist religious enthusiasm, to be a drag on science as well. And it was quite consistent of communism, also, to turn Confucian scorn into communist indulgence.

Indulgence, however, is something that a superior dispenses. There could be no question of Taoism renewing claims to pre-eminence. For science, the saving title that restored the Taoist reputation, had become an ideal of communists in a context of anti-traditionalism, both anti-Confucian and anti-Taoist. The communists had to feel, first, that they had succeeded in crushing Taoism, that it was now a thing of the past. Then it could have its place in a gallery of national achievements, its *early* place, with *early* science, while Marxists took over these latter days. When Taoism (and other products of the past) could be smoothed out of life and into a still museum, the communists would own the living present. Only when Taoism was exorcized from history—that is, from a claim to affect the future—could it be put back in history; and then it was really back, to a place of harmless honour in the people's past.

In short, Marxist relativism makes Taoism at best a progressive force in a historical stage. It must be an anachronism in the present, and the régime suppresses Taoist claims to be accepted now on grounds of absolute value. Communist policy is quite in line with communist interpretation: contemporary Taoists have been given the spades to dig their grave in history. A Taoist Association exists. What is it to do? It decided in 1961 to compile the history of the Taoist religion. It took charge of Taoist monuments. And so the Taoist temples, no longer active and therefore no longer nests of 'deceivers', have ceased to be 'feudal' in the sense of moralistic epithet; they are feudal just in the nomenclature of 'scientific history'. A temple is not a disgrace, but an antique. Communists, instead of exhorting the masses to crush the infamy, urge them to preserve the relics. That is crushing enough.

Buddhism: Between Foreign and Domestic

When Buddhism first came to China, Taoist terms were borrowed to convey certain Buddhist ideas. When the Taoist church began to spread, it copied some Buddhist ecclesiastical forms. The peasants drew on both religions for popular amalgams. The destinies of Buddhism and Taoism under the communists could not be very different.

The curators were waiting for both. Buddhism, culturally richer and more sophisticated, has been, if anything, more attentively restored. But the Buddhist restoration, like the Taoist, was not to life. It was historical restoration, an invitation to see it as it was, and to leave it, then, in the past tense. Chinese Buddhism, watched and warded in a museum-like silence, is hardly likely ever to speak again.

Therefore, iconoclasm in the literal sense is far from the communist tactic. Instead, they try to save the *bodhisattvas* in the Tun-huang* caves (while rapping the imperialist plunderers who in the bad old days had carried some of them off). These and similar monuments were produced by the people.

---

* Tun-huang, an oasis at the western end of China's Great Wall, was once a famous Buddhist centre, through which passed the caravan routes across Central Asia to Persia and Afghanistan. For a description of the great Buddhist caves adorned with frescoes and its hidden library, see Sir Aurel Stein, *On Ancient Central Asian Tracks*, Macmillan, London 1933.

They were the fruits of labour. One can set aside the politics and religion of the patrons. Under the labour theory of value, the religious values of the Buddhist symbols quietly seep away.

Religious personalities remain, and they go through ritualistic charades at a few selected sites. They staff the Chinese Buddhist Association, which is as tame as its various Christian and Taoist counterparts. Like them, and like the 'democratic parties' in the political field, the Association exists to praise the communists from the outside (the highest accolade), to bear witness to the fact that the revolution is not over, and to give the world a spectacle of communist patience and forbearance. It publishes a monthly periodical, *Modern Buddhism*. It preaches a doctrine so modern that almost anything especially Buddhist has gone out of it. All that remains is the historically significant, aesthetically valuable, religiously drained antiquities.

That is, the official Buddhists agree with the state authorities that Buddhism had become corrupt. Since feudalism and capitalism caused the rot, communism should be welcomed. The monastic life, accordingly, has been laid in ruins. The ban was the Communist Party's, denouncing monks as parasites who should be turned out to work, not left to exploit the land and live on others. But the voice of rationalization was the Buddhist Association's, which approved the attack on monasticism—as a vindication of the Buddhist ideal of mercy.

Whether or not Buddhists have the heart, they certainly have no voice to praise a Buddhist saviour. Like everyone else for his own association, they only have praise for the Communist Party, the saviour of Buddhists. But communism, which the Buddhists prudently call a cure for corruption, is rather a quietus. For the communists hold that feudalism and capitalism, far from being corrupting intruders, were really of the essence of Buddhism, and the church has no future. That is why Buddhist eyes have been directed to the past. What this religion awaits in China is not a cure, but a host of curators.

Thus, there is a good deal of editing and publishing of old Buddhist texts. An encyclopaedia of Buddhism is being compiled. The state is a friendly patron—this is to be the last word. Quite the last. Many monuments in Peking and elsewhere, especially the famous early Buddhist site, the White Horse Temple of Loyang, have been carefully restored. And a few temples and monasteries have even been left a roster of monks, to go through the traditional rounds. A complete museum needs that last touch of period authenticity.

Tourists like it, both foreign and domestic. The foreign appeal of Buddhism is something else which distinguished it from Taoism in the state's attentions. Taoism, as a philosophical and aesthetic influence, had affected other countries in history, especially Japan. However, as a religious body, Taoism has been a Chinese affair exclusively (though with strains passing into Indo-Chinese cults), and foreign interest in the Taoist question could only be slight. But Buddhism arose in India, and its adherents are still important in moulding Southeast Asian opinion. Therefore, the Buddhist museum-life, though it was called forth primarily by the cultural revolution, stayed to serve national diplomacy.

As far as India was concerned, Buddhism had long been a matter of history, so the Chinese contriving of Buddhist death-in-life could not offend; at a time when Chinese cared about blandishments to India, a common Buddhist past seemed a pleasant neighbourly bond. As for Ceylon, Burma, and other nations still Buddhist in the present, they might possibly be persuaded that it was Buddhist life they saw, and that China was respectful. A museum, after all, is a highly respectable place.

Islam: Between Ethnic and Religious Factors

Islam, another religion well represented in China, has of course, like Buddhism, a great following outside China. Still, China had once been a true centre of Buddhism, while it was always remote from the centres of Islam. And Islam did not, like Buddhism, have an all-pervasive influence on Chinese culture.

Accordingly, although a sort of patronage of Buddhists had had its uses in the Asian policy of Communist China, the Mohammedans could not be treated in the same way. Buddhism, more thoroughly 'Chinese' in its place in Chinese history (in spite of its Indian origins), was a 'Han', a national religion. But Islam, though it had millions of ethnically 'Han' adherents, had long been a Chinese 'Central Asian problem'. Even Chinese Mohammedans, not members of minority Turkic groups or the like, were seen as outsiders, often in terrible combat with the Chinese state. Compared to their 'people's tradition' good will toward the anti-state tendencies of historical Taoists or Buddhists, the communists have made only the faintest efforts to appreciate the Mohammedan risings. For Mohammedans did, and Buddhists did not, raise the spectre of internecine national struggle (*class* struggle would have been all right), and Islam became a political question. A Buddhist 'religion' under communist auspices might be politically useful externally, for impressing foreign peoples. But a Mohammedan 'people' in Communist China could be politically dangerous internally; hence, bonds with foreign co-religionists were rather to be discouraged.

Where Buddhism had an ethnic connotation on the Mohammedan model, as in Tantric, Lamaist Tibet or Inner Mongolia, there, of course, communist indulgence to Buddhism ended. It was not 'people's' there, as Buddhism might be flattered, retrospectively, in its gentry-Confucian historical milieu—but unregenerately 'feudal'. And what the communists devised for it not death-in-life, but death.

The sentence on Islam in China cannot be as harsh as that. While Islam, so potentially divisive within the nation, is not to be encouraged, it may not be peremptorily destroyed. For the open destruction of Islam would be needlessly divisive at the international level, in any Afro-Asian bloc. While China seems ready to alienate possible allies for presumably compelling national reasons, there is no sense in borrowing trouble. And so Islam remains in quarantine, but not yet certified dead.

In life, it remains officially unpopular. Precisely because Chinese Buddhism can be relativized historically to the past of the Chinese people, attention can be paid in the present to fine old Buddhist texts. These are presumed to be dead to the present, uninspiring now. Therefore, as historically *significant*, but as only *historically* significant, they are entitled to the fond care that museum keepers lavish. The communists feel that, on the whole, they can trust people with a new edition of the Lotus Sutra: they would read it as antiquarian.

Islam, however, cannot be relativized to the past of the Chinese people—only to that of a still refractory group—and it has a contemporary significance. The Koran may still claim to divert minds from their proper concerns in the present, the Marxist-Maoist revelations. And so Islamic scripture may not be guarded in the museum of restorations. Buddhism can be buried, with a eulogy; Islam has still to be cut down, with precious little praise.

Conclusion

In Africa, Islam is still a proselytizing religion. In China, it has been a long time since it tried to persuade, and its part in Chinese intellectual history has been negligible. Islam confronts the communists with only a problem of outer control, not the internal problem of Chinese continuity. Christian influence, on the other hand, and the secular Western values that accompanied it, seriously engaged the modern Chinese intellectual world, and complicated the attrition of Confucianism. How were men to arrange for its dignified expiry? How were they to save China from a seeming intellectual conquest, and keep it on the rails of a continuous Chinese history?

The communists mean to save their history by using an idea of history. As ostensibly scientific moderns, post-mediaeval or post-Confucian, they claim the future for their history at least as much as Europeans do: the latter, indeed, in their eyes, are not as post-mediaeval or post-Christian as they ought to be. And just as the chances of Christianity in China were affected by the Chinese inner intellectual struggle, so Taoism and Buddhism and the popular cults are affected. In a grudging way, Marxist history ennobles them. They make an alternative Chinese history (which Christianity could never do) to weigh against the class-tainted Confucian great tradition. But they not only make a history, in the new communist reading. They lie stranded in history, put out of their modern misery by being consigned to the past. As a communist, the Chinese communist is ready enough to bid farewell to religion. As a Chinese, for the Chinese specimens, he may stretch to hail and farewell. But still, farewell.

CHAPTER THREE

POLITICS AND ECONOMICS IN CHINESE EDUCATION

C. T. HU

The Chinese experiment in education is a unique topic for case study as it sheds light on the intricate relationship between education and national development. In a broad sense the communist transformation of China may be regarded as an educational task, because the Party's long-range objectives—be they political or economic—cannot be reached without first re-educating the people. China's educational programme is an integral and crucial part of an enormous effort to remake a nation and reshape its society. The destiny of a quarter of the world's population is of world-wide importance; and in any study of China's great problems present-day education development is a key to our understanding of a whole nation in transformation.

In the narrow academic sense, China's educational experiment, by its magnitude and wide ramifications, interests the learned community. Whether it is considered by administrators, educational psychologists or specialists in adult education, the Chinese educational scene invariably offers several features of unusual interest.

Though the Chinese have turned their backs on their traditional pattern of education, their past culture still influences them. Though they declare themselves students of Soviet experience, they are conscious of the vast differences in cultural heritage, stages of development and objective conditions which make the Soviet model applicable only in part to China. After condemning Western education as a mere instrument of the so-called ruling groups and thus decadent, they do strive to catch up with the West in science and technology. The Chinese

communists are determined to find their own answers to the
problems of education and national construction. Since many
of their problems are common to underdeveloped countries,
their experiment assumes great importance, both positive and
negative, in its international implications.

The true significance of the Chinese educational reform,
though far from complete, has to be studied in terms of the
concrete objectives laid down by the state. Let us therefore
begin by examining the general as well as the specific objectives
of education, as formulated by the Party and adopted by the
state, and follow up with an analysis of the various means
employed.

The high degree of state control is the most outstanding and
crucial element in the entire educational scene of China, and
its proper appreciation will help to read correctly the educational
balance sheet. State control of education is a part of the
totalitarian character of contemporary Chinese society:

> Totalitarianism is, indeed, the dominant theme of contemporary Chinese
> national life. . . . By insisting on Party leadership in education, the
> régime is able to pursue its educational goals with a singleness of purpose
> and degree of effectiveness unprecedented in Chinese history. Through
> the use of modern means of communication, the power of the central
> government is felt in every corner of the vast country, and the educational
> programs adopted by the Party hierarchy are implemented with all speed
> and unquestioning faith by a growing army of militant and disciplined
> Party members.[1]

With this in mind, we may now examine the political and
economic aspects of contemporary education within the
framework of the Party's objectives.

The Political Aspect of Education

To the communists, political ideology is both a means and
an end of revolution. If, prior to 1949, the teachings of Marx,
Engels, Lenin and Stalin—as interpreted by Mao—were
employed as a political weapon for the revolutionary struggle,
since 1949, these teachings (which collectively make up the
ideological framework), have formed the very basis upon

which education rests. The political objective of education, therefore, may be said to be the universal acceptance of communist ideology by the people. In order to achieve this, the communists have resorted to a variety of methods, which in their positive and negative aspects are closely interrelated.

Among the measures adopted, the introduction of Marxism-Leninism-Maoism into schools at all levels is very significant, by reason of the exclusive nature of this form of political education. Whatever its label—be it Marxism-Leninism, dialectical materialism, political economy, or simply politics—political education predominates in the school curricula; it is taught by trusted Party men, and the student's performance is judged thereby. All educational problems are treated as problems of politics, hence the slogan 'Let politics take command'. All successes are attributed to the correct handling of politics, while unsatisfactory conditions are, as a rule, blamed on a lack of understanding of political issues. All advances and retreats on the educational front are in terms of politics.

The exact ratio of political courses to the overall curriculum varies from level to level and from institution to institution. At the very top, the Institute of Marxism-Leninism, certain parts of the People's University, the Academy of Socialism and similar institutions are devoted to communist political theory and the training of political theoreticians; they are entirely politically-oriented schools. In comprehensive universities, technical institutes, normal schools, full-time secondary schools and the like, political instruction is always, in the formal structural sense, a significant part of the curriculum with informal but equally demanding political activities of all sorts, from which none is exempt. Though the titles of political courses and the way they are taught may vary considerably, ideological moulding through political education forms the core of Chinese communist education.

This great stress on politics in education appears for instance in the teaching plan of a spare-time school established for workers in a manufacturing and repair plant near Peking. Of

nine courses given over a period of two school years, with a
total of 768 class hours, politics take up 112 hours, exceeded
only by the course on machine spare parts—by six hours.[2]
In November 1959, the Ministry of Construction Engineering
called a conference to draw up an improved plan for secondary
technical schools, and the first decision taken called for more
instruction in Marxism-Leninism, requiring 300 and 400 class
hours for three-year and four-year institutions respectively.[3]
Extra-curricular activities of a clearly political nature are
constantly emphasized; participation in them and the degree
of enthusiasm displayed are important criteria whereby the
political consciousness of a student is judged. This in turn
determines the standing of each student within not only the
institution but also society as a whole. Such activities include
political demonstrations of all types, participation in productive
and what is called socially beneficial labour, in ordinary sessions
of political discussion, meetings of criticism and self-criticism,
anti-rightist campaigns, 'heart-surrendering' sessions, and
innumerable other movements. The degree of political
consciousness is equated with political reliability, which is the
single most important factor in the upward or downward
grading of individuals. In educational institutions of all levels,
political reliability or the lack of it determines the position
and treatment of teachers, and the future of students, both in
terms of further opportunities to receive education and to be
assigned work.

Red and Expert

With this stress on politics, the communists always demand
that students become both 'red and expert'. To ensure Party
leadership, the former educators have been gradually but
steadily removed, and veteran Party cadres, many with no other
qualifications than their Party cards, were appointed in their
place—on the ground of their higher degree of political
consciousness and their ability to implement the educational

directives from above. The following report gives an idea to what extent this has been carried out:

In Anhui province, Party committees on all levels have assigned a large number of Party cadres to various types of schools, where they are assuming positions of leadership. The cadres thus assigned number over ten thousand. To the five institutions of higher education, in addition to the newly established University of Anhui, the Party has assigned forty cadres who have taken up such positions as Party committee secretaries, presidents, deans, curriculum directors, general affairs chiefs, and Party secretaries for the departments. All schools have been setting up Party committees. 1,325 Party cadres have been assigned to 768 secondary schools to become principals, vice-principals, Party committee secretaries, and directors of academic and general affairs. 729 secondary schools now have principals who are Party members, representing 93·6 per cent of all secondary schools. More than 9,000 Party members have been appointed principals of primary schools. Moreover, an increasing number of teachers and school staff have been selected to become members of the Party.[4]

This trend in administration is also noticeable in the teaching personnel. The communists have followed the policy of accelerating the process of replacing the old with the new by discouraging the old from staying on and encouraging the young to take over. Thereby, the proportion of communist-educated teachers has steadily increased, partly because of the education expansion, and more so for political considerations. In Peking, in eight institutions of higher education, including the University of Peking and Tsing Hua University, the proportion of young communist-trained teachers was forty-seven per cent of the total by 1961.[5] In Tsing Hua, one of the leading institutes of technology, the overwhelming majority of new members of the faculty are products of communist higher education, who make up eighty per cent of the whole faculty.[6] Ninety per cent of the young teachers are reported to have joined either the Communist Party or the Young Communist League.[7]

The position of the 'old' teachers inherited from the past depends largely on their political acceptability to the Party, limited, however, by the régime's need of their services. Those with special qualifications in science and technology, by virtue of the less controversial nature of their work and the greater need for their service, enjoy a relatively higher degree of political tolerance, although, in times of agitation, this forbearance often disappears. Teachers in the humanities and social sciences are under constant pressure to engage in political study and to teach within the approved ideological framework.

In terms of politics, the students may be classified in three general categories: a minority who are convinced of the correctness of the Party line and actively work for the Party; the majority who acquiesce in the present state of affairs and seek to take advantage of this educational opportunity; and a minority who either openly or secretly object to political interference in education and often suffer for their views.[8]

This emphasis on politics in education has not brought about the ideological uniformity desired by the communist leaders, but through Party control, there is no longer any substantial form of actual or potential challenge to its leadership in education. This, however, was achieved at a high price of lower academic standards. The padding of the administration personnel by Party cadres, who are usually incapable of teaching, and the 'raising' of certain teachers to administrative positions as a political reward, have laid heavier responsibilities on the remaining teaching staff and increased difficulties in school operation.[9] The unduly great stress on politics has meant, in many cases, improper use of available personnel, thereby debasing the quality of instruction and wasting already limited talents. Intellectually, an extreme concern with political correctness on the part of the intelligentsia has had a stultifying effect on education, since it makes a teacher reluctant to lecture and write in a creative manner. One writer has thus referred to a 'politically doubtful' publication as a time bomb in such an intellectual climate.[10] Another factor in the lowering of academic standards has been the putting of teachers and students to do productive manual labour.

Importance of Scholarly Endeavours

It would be incorrect to say that the communists in their obsession with politics in education are not aware of its consequences. In 1958, the year of the Great Leap Forward, Liu Shao-ch'i cautioned against rash action by Party cadres in education, for, 'if not properly handled, the educational reform is liable to result in the lowering of the quality of education'.[11] Despite this, however, unrelenting efforts were made to consolidate Party control of education without which, so they reason, achievement of its objectives in every respect would be put in jeopardy. During the 'blooming and contending' campaign in 1957, when political pressure was temporarily lifted, many educators and students openly challenged the role of the Party in education and demanded the withdrawal from schools of Marxism-Leninism and of Party organizations. Confronted with such scathing criticisms, the Party brought the 'blooming and contending' to an abrupt end and adopted a series of measures to suppress its critics and to consolidate its own authority. The anti-rightist campaign was the Party's formal retort to its critics and to the dissatisfied, thereby regaining a firmer control of education.[12]

The communists do realize, however, that Party control and stress upon the 'redness' of students cannot in themselves raise educational standards and give China the trained manpower needed for national development. There is evidence of a conflict between being red and being expert and so, sure of its position, the Party since 1959, has again emphasized the importance of scholarly work. Liu Shao-ch'i warned against leaping forward in education without proper grasp of the objective conditions.[13] In 1961, vice-premier Chen Yi, in a public speech, said that it is incorrect to stress political ideology at the expense of academic standards, inasmuch as politics in the broad sense enters all constructive activities, and the national development demands trained personnel in all fields.[13] Nieh Jung-cheng, another vice-premier, also cautioned against 'redness' without substance in education.[14]

In recent years, the pendulum seems to have swung back to stress academic achievement. Political activities have become less intensive and frequent; teachers have been exhorted to concentrate on teaching and research; students have been encouraged to acquire substantive knowledge and practical skill. The catastrophic consequences of the Great Leap Forward which have adversely affected all aspects of Chinese national life, are responsible for this change. On the educational front, besides lowering of academic standards, the insistence upon ideological uniformity has caused rigidity of thought, mental stultification, and the 'middle stream' mode of thinking on the part of students.[15] This is the price the communists paid for the Party's absolute control of education in the name of politics and the silencing of their critics at least for the time being.

Economic Considerations

The intimate relationship between education and economic advancement is easily the most readily appreciated factor in social construction. In economic terms, the lack of trained personnel renders the task of economic construction difficult, irrespective of the amount of natural wealth. Personnel means human resource, which can only be developed by long and arduous training. Advances on the educational front are predicated upon the general level of economic welfare, hence the average number of years of schooling in a given society is directly related to that society's productivity, as reflected in national and personal incomes.

In denouncing Chinese education of the past, the communists have frequently resorted to the argument that it had failed to meet the economic needs of present society, and was responsible for its economic backwardness. To make education serve at all times the economic needs of China, the communists have adopted a series of measures related to economic necessities.

Their educational planning is made possible by the totalitarian character of the régime and more specifically by the high degree of Party control. Very little is left to local or individual initiative; the Party pursues its educational goal within a still larger plan for economic development. In annual state budgets, there appear not only monetary appropriations for education but also the number of students to be enrolled at all levels, including literacy classes. The degree of preciseness in planning, however, has fluctuated during the past decade or so. Prior to 1953, the first year of the First Five-Year Plan, an outline of educational planning was drawn up in accordance with the Party's basic policies. During this initial period, great efforts were in the direction of an overall reorganization of educational institutions, especially those of higher learning.[16] A good number of schools, which they considered feudalist and imperialist, were abolished or absorbed into other institutions, and new ones were established in different parts of the country. The education plan however called for consolidation and reorganization in step with the national economic plan of recovery and rehabilitation, the First Five-Year Plan.

With the advent of 1953, in keeping with the larger economic plans, education was further expanded. It became increasingly more elaborate in detail. From one billion and eight hundred million *yüan* in 1953 its budget gradually rose to two billion and three hundred million *yüan* in 1956.[17] What with appropriations for cultural and health purposes, education from 1953 took approximately 13½ per cent of the total national budget, although, in absolute monetary terms, the annual increase was about ten per cent.[18] It was due to the increased number of schools and students in the overall plans. By means of an extremely complex system, numerous government and educational organizations planned the educational requirements of the period of construction, as part of the economic plan with long and short-range specifications. For each academic year, the educational plan specifies the number of students to be enrolled at all levels, what new schools and types of schools are to be established, the extent to which existing institutions are to be expanded, the distribution of students among the various fields of specialization, and the assignment of graduates at different levels.

A Programme of Enormous Dimensions

An educational plan that involves tens of millions of people and hundreds of government, industrial, agricultural, and educational organizations poses immense problems. Until the latter part of 1962, educational development was subordinated to economic considerations to such a degree that it created difficult problems of a new sort. According to the 1960 preliminary estimate of the national economic plan, in 1961 the industrial sector of the Chinese economy would require a further 200,000 technicians of advanced and middle level; and yet in 1960 the number of graduates expected from the higher and secondary institutions was not more than 130,000.[19] In the educational plan of 1961, therefore, 280,000 students were to be sent to institutions of higher education, and a proportionately greater number to secondary schools.[20] Since the available number of candidates fell below these requirements, a nationwide campaign was launched to 'mobilize' secondary school graduates and others with equivalent qualifications. This naturally lowered immediately the academic levels in the institutes of higher education. Moreover the practice of elevating secondary schools to college level, known as 'wearing a hat', became widespread and also depressed the standards. In 1961, the number of schools of higher education was over 700, or more than a threefold increase over two years before, a task adversely affecting the general quality of education.[21]

Grandiose economic plans carried out by radical methods made more heavy demands on education after 1958 (the first year of the Second Five-Year Plan). Early in 1960 an editorial of the *People's Daily* said that, within a period of seven to ten years, China would need one million ranking agricultural technicians, though in 1960 there were no more than 170,000.[22] The Party organ exhorted all communes, industrial and commercial enterprises, and government agencies to establish all types of technical institutes, in the spirit of the Great Leap Forward. The mushrooming of schools, many in name only, was the result. Since the Great Leap movement was launched on a nation-wide scale and included all activities, education further drew on the national manpower and materials and added to the chaos, waste and fatigue all round. The Leap has had catastrophic economic and other consequences, and in the revision of economic plans, educational planning suffered a series of changes. Schools at all levels went through a process of consolidation, a large number of inefficient institutions were abolished; more consideration was given to their teaching personnel and greater efforts were made to create an atmosphere of normalcy in learning. Private initiative in educational activities is once again allowed. Temporarily at least, rigid planning has given way to a somewhat more rational and programmed development of education.

A case in point is a directive of the National Planning Commission, issued in 1959, where the principle was laid down that the assignment of graduates of higher institutions should be on a rational and priority basis, and that the needs of education must take precedence over those of production.[23] The communists seem to understand now that the educational front cannot advance by planning alone, and education should not be entirely subordinated to economic considerations.

Education and Productive Labour

Another principle is to link productive labour with education. The Resolution on the People's Communes, adopted by the Central Committee of the Chinese Communist Party in December 1958, stated that 'the principle of combining education with productive labour must be carried out thoroughly in all schools, without exception'.[24] By this means the social and other distinctions between brain and physical work were to be eliminated, basic knowledge to be acquired through practical work, education to be developed and thereby Chinese society modernized in 'greater, faster, better and more economical' manner.

The principle was interpreted by Po I-po, chairman of the National Economic Commission, to mean: *(a)* the introduction of the half-study half-work system, which requires all schools of higher and secondary education to establish factories and farms; *(b)* the transformation of schools with productive facilities into self-sufficient or nearly self-sufficient educational units; and *(c)* student participation in productive labour for a stipulated period of time after graduation.[25]

In full-time schools, the common practice is known as the '1–3–8' system: one month vacation, three months productive labour, and eight months study. The pattern of distribution of labour time varies according to types of schools and different fields of specialization. Thus, in higher institutions of technology with a course lasting five years, in a total of 260 weeks, 52 weeks are set aside for productive labour, evenly distributed among the first four school years, with an average of 13 weeks per year; the fifth year students being exempted from labour obligations. During the period assigned for labour, students are required to perform 36 hours of productive labour each week, while 18 hours are reserved for class work. On the other hand, during study periods, four hours of non-industrial labour each week are expected of all students.[26] The types of labour performed vary considerably, depending upon the location, nature, level, and economic needs of individual schools. A report on the 1958 exhibition in Peking (which showed the 'great advances' achieved through combining education with productive labour), describes two major types of labour performed by students. One type may be referred to as specialized labour which takes advantage of the special training of students. Students of geology for example will go prospecting for long periods of time in distant parts of the country; agronomists will work on farms; economics majors will do market research; and engineering students will work in factories of different kinds. The other type which involves the overwhelming majority of students, pertains to large-scale economic projects. According to statistics compiled from information supplied by twenty provinces, municipalities, and autonomous regions, 21,100 schools of all levels constructed 14,400 furnaces, and produced one and one-half million tons of steel in 1958.[27] In Liaoning province, 300,000 college and secondary school students, representing 95 per cent of the total student body, put in altogether 8 million days during the latter part of 1958 and early 1959 working on such public projects as irrigation and water conservancy, building of factories, and opening up virgin lands.[28] As to primary school children, the same Resolution on People's Communes stated that 'children above the age of nine may take part in some labour to an appropriate extent so as to acquire the habit of work in childhood and improve their physical and mental development; but full attention must be paid to the health of the children'.[29] The principle of combining education with productive labour has been 'thoroughly' carried out 'without exception' in full-time schools.

Agricultural Education

With the magnitude of present day educational tasks and the paucity of resources, the communists established, in addition to regular full-time schools, an extremely great number of half-work half-study institutions, among which the agricultural middle school is by far the most numerous and important. By 1960, after a period of two years, 30,000 agricultural middle schools had come into existence, enrolling almost 3 million students or 27 per cent of the total in junior middle schools.[30] These middle schools admit children between the ages of thirteen and seventeen, who have completed their primary education but have not advanced to regular junior middle schools. After three years' training in forestry, fishery, or animal husbandry, and agricultural science, they become junior members of an army of agricultural technicians. To appreciate the significance of this type of half-work half-study school, it should be remembered that China has now 37 million young people between thirteen and sixteen years of age, and that full-time middle schools can enroll no more than 8 million students.[31] The educational role of such half-time schools is therefore likely to become increasingly important in the foreseeable future.

The communists claim that there are several advantages in rapidly developing half-time agricultural schools. Educationally, these schools pave the way for the gradual universalization of lower secondary education; technically they provide agriculture with skilled workers; economically they make full use of the productive capacity of pupils about to become manfully productive; and in monetary terms, the annual cost to the state per pupil is only ten per cent of that of the full-time middle school, while the cost to families is only small.[32] Understandably, self-sufficiency is held up as the major goal for all half-time schools and the impact on the rural economy will be considerable.

A third type of school, in which the principle of combining education with labour is observed, are the spare-time schools. They are established within communes, industrial plants, mining enterprises, and other productive units. The subjects taught range from literacy drills to productive skills of all kinds. They eradicate illiteracy among young adults and later train them in basic skills. Since all participants have regular work to do and are wage-earners, they receive a certain amount of time off each day or week for their education. The spare-time schools represent, therefore, a form of in-service training, and have become very popular in the recent past. According to one report, eight provinces and municipalities, including Shanghai, Hopei and Peking, had by the middle of 1959 employed 21,000 full-time and 83,000 part-time instructors, and in Tientsin the number of these instructors more than doubled in less than a year.[33] Abiding by the principle of 'letting all who are capable of teaching be teachers', these schools have made full use of available human and material resources, thereby keeping the cost to a minimum. Like the agricultural middle schools, the spare-time schools of various kinds assume increasingly greater responsibilities in the popularization of education; they supplement the full-time schools which, though also on the increase, are far too few to meet the nation's economic demands.

A clearly political overtone exists in this combination of education with productive labour. The ultimate goal of education has been declared by the communists to be the creation of a generation of the Socialist Man, capable of building a 'socialist' society in the spirit of the proletariat. To combine education with productive labour is, as the slogan goes, to proletarianize the intellectuals and intellectualize the proletariat.

Concluding Remarks

A few general observations should be made about the Chinese educational development up to the present time. First, the régime is well aware of the paramount importance of education, either for the negative purpose of destroying the old or the positive purpose of creating the new. Hence there is a national commitment to education, dedicated to the three-fold purpose of nationalism, popularism, and scientism. In this regard, the communists are aided by the time-honoured Chinese tradition which considers education as the surest avenue to personal and social advancement. Second, like the pattern of economic development, education in Mainland China has gone through the several stages of rehabilitation, expansion, retrenchment, and consolidation, with less emphasis on politics, administrative decentralization, and a rational approach to productive labour. Quality recently received precedence over quantity. Third, education is popularized on an unprecedented scale. The half-time and spare-time schools, though qualitatively inferior, are at least partially meeting the urgent needs in a period of transition. With so large a number of people receiving education in one form or another, the cultural and technical level of China as a nation is bound to go up. The political and economic implications are foreseeable. Finally, given the ideological framework and the intellectual climate now prevailing, the development of education will still be subordinated to political and economic considerations more than elsewhere in the world. From a long-range viewpoint, ideological rigidity and cultural isolation, if allowed to persist, will hold up progress; but as education is a double-edged weapon, its popularization, whatever the degree of control, opens up new horizons and rises to new aspirations, thereby putting in question in the minds of the people the very ideology and the politico-economic system under which the Chinese now live on the Mainland.

NOTES

[1] C. T. Hu (ed.), *Chinese Education under Communism*, Bureau of Publications, Teachers College, New York 1962, p. 43.

[2] *Journal of Peking Normal University* (1959) 1: 73.

[3] *Kuang-ming Daily* [*Jih-pao*], 2 November 1959.

[4] *People's Daily* [*Jen-min Jih-pao*], 30 March 1959.

[5] *China News Release*, 27 November 1961.

[6] *Kuang-ming Daily*, 18 November 1959.

[7] *Ibid.*

[8] These observations are made on the basis of extensive interviews in Hong Kong with university and secondary school students who left the Mainland in recent years.

[9] *Wen-hui Daily*, Shanghai, 11 June 1957.

[10] *Wen-hui Daily*, Shanghai, 22 November 1959.

[11] *Kuang-ming Daily*, 16 January 1959.

[12] See representative articles in *China Youth News*, Peking, 24 June 1957; *People's Daily*, 18 June 1957.

[13] *Kuang-ming Daily*, 20 November 1959.

[14] *Hong Kong Times*, 19 October 1961.

[15] *Kuang-ming Daily*, 7 June 1959.

[16] Lin Feng's speech to the conference of educational and cultural advanced workers, *Wen-hui Daily*, Hong Kong, 4 June 1960.

[17] The figure for 1951 was 813 million which is illustrative of the sharp increase during the First Five-Year Plan. See *Statistical Work*, **12,** June 1956.

[18] *Hong Kong Times*, 16 August 1956.

[19] *People's Daily*, 11 January 1960.

[20] *People's Daily*, 4 June 1960.

[21] *Hong Kong Times*, 21 April 1961.

[22] *People's Daily*, 11 January 1960.

[23] *People's Daily*, 16 July 1959.

[24] *Sixth Plenary Session of the Eighth Central Committee of the Communist Party of China*, Foreign Languages Press, Peking 1958, p. 38.

[25] *Kung-shang Daily*, Hong Kong, 14 May 1959.

[26] *People's Daily*, 27 April 1959.

[27] *Education* Semi-Monthly, **21,** 1958, p. 12.

[28] *Kung-shang Daily*, 14 May 1959.

[29] *People's Daily*, 16 July 1959.

[30] *People's Daily*, 16 March 1960.

[31] Lu Ting-yi's letter to the Propaganda Department of the Party organization in Kiangsu, *China Youth News*, 23 March 1959.

[32] *People's Daily*, 16 March 1960.

[33] *Workers' Daily*, Peking, 29 May 1959.

CHAPTER FOUR

THE ROLE OF MASS MEDIA IN CHINA

HUGH HOWSE

Cultural and Historical Background

To assess the extent to which Chinese experience in the field of mass media can serve developing countries, it is necessary first to note certain unique features of China, her society and her past.

The immense size of China imposed on all who would rule it the dual problem of unification and control. In the third century B.C., when China was divided by the rival kings of the Warring States, its first emperor, Ch'in Shih Huang 秦始皇 (d. 210 B.C.) won his right to his Imperial title by uniting the country. In his ruthless enforcement of the strict laws of his own state over the other states, he introduced draconian measures to consolidate unity of his empire and gave particular attention to the media of communication in his day. First, he hastened to standardize the written language, a move which incidentally proved to be one of the most effective, unifying factors in Chinese culture down the centuries. Shortly afterwards, he controlled the ideas which could be communicated by ordering all books preaching doctrines other than those approved by the governing officials of the state to be burned.

The process of unification was further consolidated—and China's frontiers expanded—under the succeeding Han dynasty whose long imprint on Chinese culture survives to this day. Under the Han emperors, the scholars and officials of the newly centralized empire became the transmitters of a new orthodoxy —the ethical and political doctrines of Confucius which formed the cement of Chinese society to the present century. The Confucian classics were the foundation of education, and success in examinations based on this classical orthodoxy became the only road to government office. Confucian doctrine firmly tied the individual to a family and political relationship. The media of communication played a key role in the achievement of this historical phenomenon. First, the standardized written language was a basic factor in the unity and continuity of this culture. Secondly, the printed word of the Confucian classics formed the content of the unifying orthodoxy. Thirdly, and most important, education was both the channel of communication as well as the means of ensuring that no other doctrine or influence likely to change the status quo could enter, disturbingly, from the world outside.

In the middle of the 19th century the West, borne on the wave of the Industrial Revolution, broke into this Chinese self-centred world with a shattering impact. Under first the military and then the cultural impact of the West, China's ossified society disintegrated like a brittle fossil. The subsequent breakdown in Chinese national cohesion was such that Sun Yat-sen, founder and father of the Chinese Republic, described the Chinese people as 'loose sand'. Throughout the hundred years of China's turmoil, from the middle of the 19th century to 1949, a wide variety of political, philosophical—and even literary and aesthetic—theories vied with each other for national acceptance. This cultural dislocation (not unlike the situation of the Hundred Schools of rival philosophies which prevailed during the era of the Warring States from 481 B.C. until three centuries later Ch'in Shih Huang put an end to them in 221 B.C.) was beyond the means of the Nationalist Party or Kuomintang 國民黨 to repair, for it had no pervasive doctrine to offer. But the Chinese Communists did have one and its ideology moreover had a strong element of built-in evangelism.

Rapid Development of the Mass Media

Against this background—to borrow Voltaire's phrase about God—it could be said that if the mass media hadn't existed, the Chinese Communist Party would have had to invent them.

They were developed with such rapidity by the Communist
Government that the casual outside observer—overlooking the
development of radio, the press and the film under the Kuomintang—might be forgiven for assuming that the Chinese Communist Party had invented mass media.

Statistics serve writers—and propagandists in particular—
like lamp-posts serve drunken men—as means of support rather
than for light. Though eschewing figures wherever possible,
I should like to give a few here (mostly from Chinese communist sources) to show how rapid this development of
the mass media has been. After ten years of communist
control, China's radio transmitting power was five times
greater than the *total* transmitting power under the Kuomintang in the twenty years from 1928 to 1947. Other media,
already far better developed than radio by the Kuomintang,
were rapidly extended. By 1956, the circulation of newspapers
was double the figure of the Chinese press in 1936, and the
corresponding figures for magazines and books for the same
period increased by ten times. In 1956 the number of film
projection units in China was 20 times the 1936 figure and the
professional drama groups had increased in that period by
2,000 units.[1] Even allowing for a traditional tendency to exag-
gerate statistics, these figures have a relative value in showing
the immense importance the Chinese Communist Party attaches to the mass media. In absolute terms, its network for
mass communication in just over fourteen years since 1949 is
quantitatively impressive. However, when one considers that
mass media were not used for broadening horizons but for
naked exploitation for narrow Party ends, the achievements
are less impressive.

Radio and Television

If the press, publications and the film were already well-
established in China, however limited in their range under the
Kuomintang, radio played little part in the lives of most

people until 1949 onwards. The few radio stations which existed previously—mainly privately owned—were in the major ports (predominantly Shanghai) and cities. The broadcasting network, which now penetrates all parts of the country, is very much the creation of the Chinese Communist Party. At its centre and head, is the powerful Central People's Broadcasting Station in Peking which is, in turn, subservient to the Bureau of Broadcasting Affairs of the State Council. In addition to the local, national and international services broadcast from the centre, there are over 100 local stations in provincial centres and major municipalities which relay parts of the central output from Peking and have their own local programmes. These local, provincial and municipal stations, in turn, have been supplemented in remote areas, if necessary, by other even more localized arrangements, for example local 'broadcasting centres', 'receiving stations' equipped with loudspeakers and 'monitoring teams' which also issue handouts of the radio broadcasts, taken down in writing. Thus no part of the country misses the message from the centre. Peking attaches such importance to its message that in 1955 it planned it should be possible for all to hear the programmes of the Central People's Broadcasting Station by 1962. In external broadcasting—begun by the Communist Government with comparatively short transmissions to overseas Chinese in 1950—China rose to third position in the world of external broadcasters in 1960 with 732 hours of broadcasting per week, predominantly directed at audiences in Asia, Africa, Latin America and the Middle East. Only the communist satellite countries all combined, followed by the Soviet Union (itself a target for China's broadcasts since February 1962) give more time on the air to their foreign broadcasts.[2]

The Party assigned to this vast broadcasting network—what the Central People's Broadcasting Station calls its function— the role of 'strengthening links between the centre and the regions, the Party, government and working people' and of 'strengthening the patriotic education of the masses'. Tactically it gives immediate, nation-wide diffusion to policy statements and official announcements from the centre as never possible before. National campaigns and mass movements engineered at the centre are immediately taken up by local stations in the provinces as discussion themes and directives. At the local level it has served the Party's short-term ends, for example, to activate land reform, to promote the formation of rural co-operatives, of communes, and to raise production to meet national and local quotas. The masses are radio lectured on every conceivable subject, at ordinary or high levels, for example, on Marxist-Leninism and Maoism (the thought of Mao Tse-tung), pig-breeding, birth control, hygiene, etc.

Most importantly, however, the radio network has been employed at all times as a means of building up pride in Chinese achievement and in spreading the gospel that it is the Chinese Communist Party which has been responsible for the national revival. Through radio the Party speaks to the whole nation; it also helps specific groups in their programmes designed for the youth, army, industrial workers and children. From the centre to the provinces and from provincial capitals to outlying areas, it has enabled the Party to convey a uniform picture of China itself and of the outside world. It has permeated the country with the Marxist-Leninism ideology as interpreted by Mao Tse-tung. In short, it has been used exactly as Ch'in Shih Huang and the Han emperors used their means of communication—in support of a centralized, unified state created on the basis of a new, uniform orthodoxy.[3]

The Chinese also see the potential of television. Plans for China's first television centre in Peking were completed in 1957 with Soviet assistance. It went into trial operation in May 1958 and began regular evening transmissions in September 1958. Since then, according to Peking Radio, over twenty television stations have been set up in other cities, particularly in industrial areas, but several are still in the trial stage. At least eight stations were operating regularly by the middle of 1962. Transmissions are for limited periods, sets are few and mainly public but good use has been made of the existing facilities in extending higher level education by establishing Television Universities in a number of cities. Although television is still in its initial stages in China, it is to be even more intensively developed than radio as a medium and in its use propaganda is obviously going to predominate.

Thus the Deputy Director of the Broadcast Research Institute in Peking at the end of 1961 said: 'An excellent instrument for propaganda and culture, television is able to penetrate into the everyday life of the people. . . television carries both sound and picture and is more complete than the radio broadcast. . . . In the field of propaganda, television has far greater advantage than other propaganda media'. The expense of setting up such a vast broadcasting network, particularly insofar as external broadcasting and television are concerned is considerable, and yet China, on the admission of her leaders, was still economically a backward country before the onset of severe economic difficulty and strain in 1960. This continued build-up in broadcasting therefore demonstrates all the more the importance the Party attaches to mass media; it also reflects an allocation of priorities which gives greater importance to the strength of the Party's voice than to fuller rations for the people's stomachs. It is an allocation of priorities which few other developing countries, if any, could afford economically, socially or politically.[4]

The Written Word and Other Media

Whilst the spoken word of radio, and even more so that of television, are new forces in Chinese society today, the written word has been the traditional bond of Chinese society and its holiness is still venerated today. The broadcasting network in China is essentially a mechanical device for transmitting information, ideas and policies initiated elsewhere—it is never used as the initial source of information. This important role belongs to the written word. One can almost hear the reverential hush when the radio, as so often happens, introduces a leading article from the Peking *People's Daily* as its main commentary, and thus reveals the basic relationship between the main mass media of radio and press. This was also clearly exposed in 1957 when the Hundred Flowers campaign released such a flood of criticism of Party dogmatism and control that the floodgates had to be quickly closed. The criticism during that campaign was mainly against the press and the Party's control over it, and much less against the radio. A teacher in the department of journalism of China People's University, thus said: 'The role of the newspaper as textbook is over-emphasized. It is always used to transmit orders from the upper echelons to the lower echelons'.[5] And a student at Peking University described the leading Chinese Communist newspaper, the Peking *People's Daily*, as 'The Great Wall sealing off the truth'.[6]

These and similar criticisms of the press made then are still largely true. A key authoritarian role is assigned to the press by the Party. 'Newspapers serve as the Party's ears, eyes, throat and tongue; they are the most powerful ideological weapon.'[7] Again, 'Our understanding is that the organic function of a newspaper is to publicize correctly the guiding principles, policies and lines of the Party and to agitate and organize all the people in the province to form a strong force and fight for the realization of the great tasks lined up by the Party for the different historical periods'.[8] These orthodox views of the function of the press flow from that very fountain-head of propaganda in China, Lu Ting-yi, chief of the Propaganda Department of the Central Committee of the Chinese Communist Party. In an address in 1957 on the occasion of the 20th anniversary of the New China News Agency, he referred to the role of journalism in the following terms: 'Journalism is the tool of the class struggle. . . . The New China News Agency issues its tens of thousands of words per day in order to educate and unite the people, expose and overthrow enemies and promote the development of the forces of socialist production'. The ever-expanding New China News Agency,[9] organized, like broadcasting, to serve China's national, provincial and international needs, is responsible for gathering, selecting and distributing news and policy items to the press and radio. Through the New China News Agency, a nation-wide uniformity of news is ensured. The biased nature of this uniformity—and the truth of the criticism already directed at the Peking *People's Daily* above—can be imagined from another point Lu Ting-yi made in his address when he emphasized that in journalism politics is all and added: 'Whether an item of news is issued quickly, delayed or suppressed must be carefully considered from a political point of view. Reporters and editors have two duties: one is to publish quickly and the other is to suppress'.

It is on these principles that a tightly-knit and tightly controlled network of papers has been established.[10] They are organized to give the Party a press coverage as nation-wide as broadcasting. There are national newspapers at the centre, headed by the Peking *People's Daily* (which prints editions in certain major cities), and their leading articles on key issues are often re-printed in all other papers the following day. There are hosts of other papers at provincial and various local levels side by side with other publications for special audiences—theoretical journals for Party cadres, youth papers and magazines, papers and magazines for intellectuals and writers, industrial workers, farmers, scientists, etc. In 1959, the Minister of Culture spoke of 1,884 kinds of newspaper in China and, as early as 1958, it was said that there was one copy of a newspaper for every 40 people as against one for every 274 in 1950.[11] By 1960, 'under the policy of operating newspapers by the whole Party', in a report made by journalists at a cultural conference we read: 'Under the direct leadership of the Chinese Communist Party Committee at various levels, the Central Government as well as the various provinces, municipalities, special administrative areas, counties, people's com-

munes, factories, mines and other enterprises have already
established a powerful, closely knit, correspondence network'.[12]
Again, as for radio, considerable expenditure has been allocated
to publications for foreign consumption which are significantly
of better quality and more brightly dressed than those circulated
within China; the quality of paper and newsprint of the latter
are as uniformly as poor as their contents are dull.

This vast network of publications and broadcasting which
penetrates the whole country is backed by many other media—
the film, literature, theatre, ballet, opera, and even songs. We
shall state here their salient points. As in broadcasting and the
press, the Party's concern has been two-fold: to expand the
technical facilities for the media and increase the volume of
their output and to subordinate them to its own ends. The
following quotation which illustrates the role of the film in
China today, is typical of the use to which all these other media
are put and the degree to which they serve, not art or even
entertainment, but predominantly the Party:

As the motion picture is one of the most popular arts and one of the
Party's most effective weapons of propaganda and education, in our film
undertakings we must necessarily put political-ideological work and the
question of creative thinking first, strengthen the Party's leadership over
the cinema, resolutely and unyieldingly implement Chairman Mao's
principles concerning literature and art and closely follow the general line
for increasing our zeal, going all out and building Socialism with 'greater,
faster, better and more economical' results.[13]

How Effective are the Mass Media?

The foregoing outline of the mass media in China and their
role under the Chinese Communist Party gives a sufficient idea
that the Party's adoption, expansion and exploitation of these
media is almost certainly the largest propaganda effort which
the world has ever seen. But is this operation applicable to
problems of mass communication in other developing countries?
What of the intensity of the effort? And setting aside questions
about the social, moral, economic and political values involved
in such a totalitarian and dogmatic approach to mass media,

has this intensive operation been successful and in what measure could it be copied in other countries?

Considered *in vacuo*, the size and intensity of the propaganda barrage directed at the Chinese people in the manner shown, it might be thought it is altogether self-defeating. This would almost certainly be the case in most countries, not accustomed to a total social and political conformity. But in China, there has been a long tradition of social, cultural and political conformity based on Confucian doctrine and enshrined in their hallowed and venerated writing. As a result, although some of the mass media are new in the mechanical sense, their use in spreading conformity is a process to which the Chinese have been long accustomed. On the whole, therefore, there has been less resistance in China than would be found in any other society in which these conditioning factors of the past do not apply.

Nevertheless during the brief campaign of the 'Hundred Flowers', criticism and later other murmurings have been heard against much of the mass media. Broadcasts were said to be dull, too full of statistics and heavy lecturing, and included too many 'calls for accumulating manure or for catching insects'.[14] The press, too, apart from the charges noted already, was described as dull and like a gramophone; many books and periodicals were considered—even by the communist press itself[15]—to be so poor in thought and style as not worth publishing. Again on Party admission,[16] most of the films produced have been acknowledged to be second grade and audiences have found them dull, shallow and of a set pattern. In 1957, many writers appealed for creative freedom and the liberty to read works dubbed 'bad' simply because they had been written before 1949 or had originated in capitalist countries. An article appeared at the time in the *Wen-yi pao* (Journal of Literature and Arts) saying that present works were not interesting enough. 'Can we lead dramatic groups as we would lead an army?' asked another writer in the same journal.[17] These and many other criticisms mark the failure of mass media at certain points and in relation to other social groups besides the intellectuals.

The Problem of the Intellectuals

The failure of mass media among the intellectuals has been conspicuous. This is worth considering, not simply because of the importance of intellectuals to any developing society, but because of its far reaching consequences. In China, the Party insists on ideological purity, on politics 'in command' everywhere, and on absolute conformity, and it has used the mass media to saturate the people's mind with these ideas. This has inhibited and virtually killed that very creativity, whether in science or the arts, that is the life-blood of a developing society. To encourage once again creativity, in 1956 Mao Tse-tung— who thought that a satisfactory stage in control and unification had been reached by then—launched the Hundred Flowers campaign under the slogan 'Let a hundred flowers bloom and a hundred schools contend'.[18] But such was the dead weight of the conformity already established by the mass media and other means,[19] that the intellectuals hesitated to come forward in word, thought or deed. Only when a direct invitation to criticize was issued in 1957—in a campaign to 'rectify' the Party—did people begin to speak up and they poured out their criticisms in floods. This, and, above all, a critical unrest amongst students, made the Party a few weeks later launch a counter campaign to stop the criticism—it was against the 'rightists' (the label attached to those who were making the criticisms). The intellectuals were again cowed into silence. The Party's mass media continues to suffer from dullness and absence of creativity, and Communist China is still without a film, a play, a novel or a poem of real artistic or literary merit. Even more serious to a developing country, the efforts of the rare and therefore highly valuable scientific and technical experts of China have been subordinated to and inhibited by the political orthodoxy—the first requirement in the Party's system of values spread through the mass media and other socio-political channels. The ill effects and the dangers of this situation, reflected in China's shortcomings in science and technology, were so apparent that, since the middle of 1961 the aim of having specialists who were 'both red and expert'— to use yet another campaign slogan of the mass media—has been dropped in favour of expertness, specialization and some stimulus to independent research and scholarship.

Another significant statement comes from Chou En-lai who, at the 1962 National People's Congress, spoke of the greater need of 'personal ease of mind' in China. But the Party's use of the mass media has not been conducive to such a desirable 'ease of mind' and, as yet, there has been no easing up in the Party's pressure. The issue of the mass media has thus been a complicating factor in the Party's dilemma of demanding total political and social conformity while the country wants an intellectual 'easing of mind' for creative development and technological progress.

Other Problems

These problems and weaknesses of the mass media are mainly recognized by the Party itself. Other problems, arising from the very success of the mass media, are not so widely realized. It is doubtful if what is to an outsider the most dangerous aspect of the use of mass media would be recognized as such by many people within China today. The greatest success of the mass media has been in the renewal of Chinese national consciousness and a revitalization of the whole nation. Through the mass media, the whole population was mobilized in a manner never possible before, in hundreds of campaigns, both local and nation-wide, from killing sparrows to 'giving one's heart to the Party', and from 'studying the thought of Mao Tse-tung' to establishing the communes. A campaign a day, one may say, kept the communists under way. We have given historical reasons why the Chinese are inured to thought control by the state. The very essence and tone of the Chinese classics, as we have seen, once performed the role of the present mass media, of impersonal exhortation towards a set pattern of socio-political behaviour.

At times, the very success of mass media campaigns created new problems. The over-enthusiasm engendered in 1958 during the euphoria of the Great Leap Forward and the establishment of the communes led to industrial waste (the 'backyard' furnaces which produced vast quantities of unusable steel), transport chaos and such a pitch of optimism about the arrival of the communist millennium, that the Party realized the dangers of being 'dizzy with success'. The intoxicating atmosphere of enthusiasm and emulation, spread by the mass media, was a significant factor in the exaggeration in 1958 of the statistics for production, which had to be scaled down to somewhere much nearer the truth. Generally, however, the Chinese Communist Party's use of the mass media has been successful in converting what had become an apathetic attitude of the public under the Kuomintang, of 'let each man sweep the snow from his own door'—to quote a Chinese saying—into one of the people's association and participation in 'mass' movements initiated at the centre. Particularly skilful has been the use of the past to benefit the present, as in the very name of the 'Hundred Flowers', or in transferring the connotation of the word 'family' from that of the narrow family system of the past to the vast 'big family' of the commune and the nation. The word 'ancestor' in its former, more limited sense is now applied to the country as a whole, *tsu-kuo* 祖國 (literally 'ancestral country') and is now a term for 'Chinahood', much used by the mass media in widespread appeals to patriotism. The mass media deliberately exploit—in radio programmes, press articles, films and plays alike—topics such as the humiliations of the 19th century and the heroic exploits of the Chinese Communist Party and the army in achieving victory and the nation's new-found unity and strength. China's abasement, in the last century down into the middle of this century, in contrast with her glorious position in the past, offered the Party unique opportunities in awakening the nation. In its appeal through mass media to the people, it invariably added that 'thanks to the leadership of the Chinese Communist Party and Chairman Mao in particular' China had made a national recovery and was now strong again. But it has also isolated China again to a far more dangerous degree than in the past.

The world presented through the eyes of the Chinese Communist Party and its mass media is one which has not changed since Lenin's day; it is one in which 'imperialism' (despite all the Asian and African states which now swell the number of independent member countries of the United Nations) is still rampant and may well need to be defeated by war (despite the horror of nuclear conflict from which most of mankind recoils). As a result, China has not only become isolated from the West (this might be understandable in light of China's experience in the 19th century) and from much of the Afro-Asian world (this too would be understandable in the light of the past when all other countries, near or far, were considered 'barbarian' by the Chinese), but even from most other countries within the communist bloc. This is the real danger China presents in the world of today—the Party has retired her behind a Great Wall which seals her off from the truth and from outside reality.[21]

The Chinese Communist Party is the architect of this new Great Wall, and the mass media are the bricks and the mortar with which it has been built. In the days of China's isolation in the 19th century a Chinese scholar-official, nurtured on the Confucian classics (as Party men today are fed on the mass media), was asked if he didn't think he might learn something by travelling abroad. He replied that one who had read the Confucian *Four Books* had nothing left to learn. In China, the wheel of history has, in many respects, not so much rolled forward as merely turned full circle. The mass media for all the spin they have given to the wheel have also acted as a brake.

Conclusion

To sum up this outline of the nature, role and effectiveness of the mass media in China: what has been built up is quantitatively impressive, but, qualitatively, leaves much to be desired. As a Party weapon, the mass media—aided by the nature of Chinese society and China's past—have been successful in mobilizing the people and in spreading a new conformity to replace the old. This very success, however, has raised as many problems as it has solved, and some of the resulting problems involve the whole world. It is therefore not surprising that other Asian countries which seek guidance or assistance from other Asian nations, to set up or improve their media of communication, turn not to Communist China but to Japan.[22] Just as Japan leads not only Asia but also most of Western Europe in some fields of industrial production and in her rate of development, she is far in the lead in Asia too in the field of mass communications. This is true not only of the technical development of the mass media but also of the quality, creativity and genuinely educational and progressive effect of their content—the very qualities which the mass media lack in China but which, in Japan, have made a significant contribution to her rapid development which has outstripped that of all other countries.

NOTES

[1] Figures mainly from Chinese press articles which were reprinted in 'The People's Handbook' *(Remin Shouce)*, 1958.

[2] At the time of writing, the United States has gone ahead of the Chinese (in autumn 1962 the Voice of America's broadcasting hours per week were 803 to Radio Peking's 778), but China is still ahead of Britain which with the BBC's 603 hours per week holds the fifth place.

[3] Naturally, radio in China provides music and entertainment for a hard-worked people and also serves educational purposes, but this is subordinate to its political role. In 1950, news and political broadcasts were 50% of the output. This decreased later to about 30% but is still the hard core of programmes around which music, plays, opera, story-telling, etc. are grouped and moreover contain indoctrination.

[4] In smaller matters of the Party's propaganda there is now some recognition of this problem of priorities. Theatrical troupes—in themselves a medium for propaganda—have long been encouraged by the Party but the Peking *People's Daily* on 27 November 1962 criticized production units for incurring large amounts of unproductive expenditure in forming theatrical troupes and their equipment.

[5] New China News Agency, 17 May 1957. See *The Hundred Flowers* by Roderick MacFarquhar, pp. 59 and 76, for an account of the press in relation to the campaign.

[6] See 'The rectification campaign at Peking University: May-June 1957' by Rene Goldman in *The China Quarterly*, 12 (October-December 1962).

[7] Article in the *Yangtze Daily*, 17 February 1959.

[8] Article in *News Front*, 1 (1959), referring to the *Honan Daily*.

[9] Recent years have seen a remarkable increase in the number of New China News Agency correspondents abroad. From 21 foreign bureaux in 1957, there are now 40. The significant increase has been in Africa and Latin America.

[10] Up to 1957, five papers were allowed a semblance of independence with a non-Party status, provided that they served Party interests like the 200 papers of the Party, then in existence. This semblance of independence disappeared after the campaign against the 'rightists' late that year.

[11] The campaign against illiteracy, begun by the Kuomintang, was rapidly stepped up by the Chinese Communist Party and literacy classes are skilfully used for indoctrination. From 1949 to 1957 the Party estimated that 22 million people had become literate. By 1960 some provincial authorities were claiming 90 per cent success in eliminating illiteracy.

[12] New China News Agency, 10 June 1962.

[13] Peking *People's Daily*, 2 February 1960, reprinted in the *China Quarterly* 2 (April-June 1960).

[14] An article in Peking *People's Daily*, 6 February 1954, entitled 'Improving the quality of radio broadcasts by strengthening the tie between radio station and the listening public', quoted in *To Change A Nation* by Franklin W. Houn, p. 172, an excellent survey of propaganda and indoctrination in China.

[15] The *New Observer*, 16 May 1959.

[16] *Red Flag*, 19 October 1961.

[17] See Roderick MacFarquhar, *The Hundred Flowers*, pp. 174–194, for a survey of the writers' criticisms.

[18] 'The Hundred Schools' is a historical reference to the period of contending philosophies which accompanied the Warring States in Chinese history. To exploit the past for present use is a constant and interesting feature of Party propaganda.

[19] Only in the previous year, a Marxist literary critic, Hu Feng, who had challenged the role of the Party in relation to literature, found himself the subject of a nationwide campaign, pressed home through the mass media and was finally arrested.

[20] To quote an example of this tendency to look backwards in the aim of generating patriotic and revolutionary enthusiasm, in the still very difficult year of 1961, the Peking *Daily Worker*, 14 October 1961, said that teams of story-tellers were touring workers' clubs, workshops and even dormitories to spread knowledge of past hardships, while workers' libraries had made special arrangements to make available books on revolutionary themes. Specially

trained teachers were also being sent to the factories to train workers to sing revolutionary songs.

[21] Mr Khrushchev's speech at the meeting of the Supreme Soviet in Moscow December 1962 attacked the Chinese, by name, for their unrealistic attitude to the world beyond their pale.

[22] The only known exceptions are Communist North Vietnam for obvious reasons and neutralist Cambodia, which takes aid from many quarters as a matter of policy.

Part II

Building for the Future:
An Economic Analysis

CHAPTER FIVE

MEASURES OF ECONOMIC PLANNING

GORDON BARRASS

For men to plunge headlong into undertakings of vast change, . . . they must have the feeling that by the possession of some potent doctrine, infallible leader or some new technique they have access to a source of irresistible power. They must also have an extravagant conception of the future . . . they must be wholly ignorant of the difficulties involved in their vast undertaking. Experience is a handicap.

ERIC HOFFER, *The True Believer* (1961)

Such is the view of a longshoreman, migratory labourer and student of mass movements, speaking of leaders who set out to change the world and lift their countries out of traditional ruts on to the road to sustained economic growth—to leap out of the Middle Ages into the twentieth century.

For China, the disruption of more than twenty years of war and civil war and a history of fragmentation had put the need for a strong central government beyond question, or indeed choice. The Chinese communists came to power, however, convinced not only that a strong central government was essential to modernize China, but also that the best means was by developing heavy industry as quickly as possible. There is little evidence that they seriously considered any other ways of modernization. Industrialism was an integral part of their revolutionary faith—which was a mixture of Marxism and nationalism. Not only would industrialization rid China of its poverty and what has been called China's 'humiliating impotence' but also, by Lenin's definition, only through industrialization and the mechanization of agriculture could China become a socialist society and so remove the social injustice of the past. Modernizing in any case posed great problems for China, but the political choice of concentrating on the development of heavy industry accentuated these problems.

China's Approach to Economic Planning

Greatly impressed by the Soviet example the Chinese communists hoped that they could lay in China the basis of a modern industrial economy by the end of the first three five-year plans (1953–1967). But the Bolsheviks' success was not due only to strong state control and the impetus of a revolutionary government. Contrary to popular belief, Russia was already the world's seventh most industrialized nation when Stalin set out to modernize it. While Russian agriculture was backward, productivity was high enough for Stalin's ruthless government to squeeze from the peasants a 'surplus' which would pay for rapid industrialization. On the other hand, the Chinese communists started with a comparatively small, if important, industrial base. Yet, even by 1952, when they had restored the pre-war level of production, they were dealing with an economy characterized by traditional peasant agriculture and overpopulation on the land. Moreover, the intense anti-imperialism of the Chinese revolution led them to cut the country off from the international market in a way the Soviet Union never was cut off. Most of China's trade was done with the Soviet bloc on not very advantageous terms.

The Chinese, nevertheless, expected to finance industrialization along Soviet lines. Production would increase, Marx had argued, if private ownership was abolished and people were paid according to the quality and quantity of their work. Everyone then would not only have to work for a living, but also would have incentives to work harder. Rent and profits which had been misused by landlords and the bourgeoisie could be turned into productive capital. The Chinese communists took this train of thought still further. They believed that by reorganizing agriculture along original lines, while investing only a small amount of capital, production could be increased sufficiently to provide the large surplus needed for industrialization. Given the sorry state of Chinese agriculture and the high nationalistic hopes of the communists it is easy to see the appeal of this concept attributed to Marx. But Marx was a theorist of the industrial world; he hated the 'idiocy' of peasant life and showed a lack of understanding when he implied that agriculture could best be treated like large-scale industry. True, large-scale organization of farming can give the state greater control; and peasants can be more easily mobilized for construction work. However, as the Chinese were to discover, large-scale farming does not do away with the need for flexibility in tending crops or the role of incentives.

Intense nationalism brought something of a saving grace to China's revolution. The Chinese people, apart from 'counter-revolutionaries' and 'exploiters', were thought of as one nation, which the Communist Party would gradually lead to 'socialism'. And, although Mao Tse-tung favoured 'a little terror', he abhored the idea of industrializing through unadulterated coercion. Peasants were given land under the land-reform programme—which was accompanied by much violence—in order to win their support. This was also meant to free them from their 'feudal fetters', before moving them into co-opera-tives (in which peasants were paid for their contribution of land, tools and labour) and collectives (in which peasants were paid only for their work). By taking over the property of the former Nationalist government, foreigners and other undesir-ables, as well as setting up their own trading agencies, the communists were able to dominate the market. By regulating taxes, wages and profits, and by their intensive political campaigns they were also able to gain a firm control over the remaining private sector of the economy. Perhaps the most virulent campaign against business was the 'five-antis' campaign of 1952. The pretext was that of a drive against bribery, tax evasion, theft of state property, fraud and theft of state econo-mic secrets.

The long revolutionary struggle had given China's leaders much faith in men and ideas. But it was an open question to what extent these should be relied upon in the process of industrialization. Behind the ever shifting Party line a great debate has gone on about the rate at which China should industrialize and how this was to be carried out. There were two groups in this debate. Firstly, there were the 'crusaders' who believed that the Chinese people could be moulded into a vast revolutionary crusade which, by its sheer force of numbers and willingness to endure hardships, could break out of backwardness and produce a surplus to invest in economic growth. The crusaders argued that the development of basic industry must go ahead relentlessly if China was not to slip from the road to socialism. Secondly, there were the 'planners', who pointed out that China's material resources were limited; they talked, like Chou En-lai at the Eighth National Congress, more cautiously of 'planning on a forward-looking and completely sound basis, to ensure a comparatively *balanced* development'. They were critical of spectacular but short-lived successes that brought chaos in their wake; mass crusades, because of their emotional nature, inevitably led to economic and political excesses.

The division between crusaders and planners (although the line was by no means clear cut) was reflected within the Chinese politburo. The Leap Forward of 1956 and the Great Leap Forward of 1958 were led by the men who head the Party machine and whose function was to make sure, through Party cadres, that the people work properly. Their critics were the men who (although members of the Party) work primarily in the machinery of government and economic planning, as distinct from the Party hierarchy. Their views were shaped by the need to plan, collect surpluses and make investment decisions. This group led the retreat from the Great Leap Forward.

Along these often contradictory lines of thought the Chinese, having restored pre-war levels of production by 1952, approached their first Five-Year Plan. The shape of things to come was anticipated in the preceding three years when the Communist Government strengthened its control over banking and foreign trade, took over most existing manufacturing and trading enterprises and set up new ones of its own. All the media of control familiar to totalitarian régimes had been applied: essential parts of foreign and indigenous private capital had been expropriated and brought under public control either directly or in the form of so-called joint enterprises; the flow of commodities was regulated by government agencies; money market and foreign exchange were kept under strict central control; and forced savings were obtained through strict rationing of consumer goods and through farm-delivery quotas imposed on grains and other agricultural products.

Having thus restored China's economic output to pre-war level, the communists were now out to harness the economy for growth beyond anything ever achieved before.

The First Five-Year Plan (1953–7)

China's first Five-Year Plan was a considerable success—even though targets were under-fulfilled, and not over-fulfilled as the Chinese claimed. The Manchurian industrial complex had been much enlarged and new industrial centres were being set up at Wuhan (in Central China) and Paotow (in Inner Mongolia). Steel output was claimed to have risen four times, electricity two and a half times, and coal output twofold. Machine tools, trucks, refined sugar and paper, among other things, were produced in China in significant quantities for the first time. But this triumph was something of a Pyrrhic victory. Not only did the strains it produced in the economy give grave warning of what development along these lines might bring, but the plan actually tended to accentuate the problems which the Party leaders later tried to solve through the Great Leap Forward.

Through a massive state investment programme the Chinese hoped to boost national income by over 7 per cent each year. With two-thirds of state investment being channelled into industry (and concentrated initially on 156 Russian designed and equipped projects) industrial production was expected to double within five years. Agriculture, on the other hand, received relatively little capital so that farm land was not significantly expanded nor traditional methods much improved. As priority was given to the production of grain, the output of crops important for light industry and exports failed to reach their targets. For all the extravagant Chinese claims, agricultural production as a whole probably did not increase by more than 3 per cent a year—or a little faster than the rise in population. Largely because of this, the growth of China's national income was held back to about 5 per cent a year.

The decision of the Chinese communists to name 1953 as the first year of the plan to some extent reflected ambition more than preparedness. Although state control of the economy had been extended considerably during the Korean War, there was no hope at that stage even of producing detailed economic plans. Both the State Planning Commission and the State Statistical Bureau had been set up at the end of 1952, but it was not until mid-1955 that they were working efficiently enough to produce a detailed plan. Not surprisingly, given the haste and the inexperience, as well as the political convictions of the leadership, China relied heavily on Soviet precedents. Most of the details of the plan (i.e. wage and tax schedules and the regulations for collectives) were hastily adapted from Soviet textbooks. This does not deny the later originality of the Chinese in dealing with problems European communists had not faced; in particular they introduced collectivization without mechanization in 1955–6, and the communes in 1958. However, the Soviet model could not be adopted in its entirety, for China started its plan with nearly all of its agricultural production, two-thirds of its trade and one-third of its modern industry still in private hands. Originally, the Chinese envisaged only a gradual process of socialization—with private enterprises still producing $12\frac{1}{2}$ per cent of modern industrial output and only half of the peasants having joined co-operatives by 1957.

The plan, although primarily concerned with state investment in the public sector, could hardly ignore such a large segment of the total economy. Taxes, profits, the system of supply of raw materials, and government purchases had to be formulated in such a way as to induce a favourable response from a large number of individual, and often small, firms. Nor were these the only spheres in which purely economic or market forces had a role. The Chinese were well aware that industrial growth was not due to large amounts of investment alone, but was highly dependent on a fluid supply of skilled labour. While political and social pressures could be and were used by the Party to move workers from one industry to another—to a degree which amounted to the administrative direction of labour—these means were supplemented by high wages to attract skilled workers into heavy industry and by rewards to encourage them to improve their performance.

The structure of the economy was not the only restraint curtailing the Chinese manoeuverability in planning. After long and bitter negotiations with the Russians the Chinese communists realized that they could expect little aid. Russian loans covered only 3 per cent of state investment under the plan, while all other Russian assistance (equipment and technicians) had to be paid out of current production, i.e. by Chinese exports to the Soviet Union. Since the plan required capital accumulation of approximately 20 per cent of the national income—and such other governmental expenses as defence, social services and administration had to be met—it was necessary to channel some 30 per cent of the national income through the budget. By the end of the plan 80 per cent of government revenue was coming from the profits and taxation of government enterprises (including the state marketing boards); 7 per cent from direct taxes; 7 per cent from taxes on joint enterprises, and the remainder from loans and savings.

The original source of most of this revenue was, of course, agriculture. Because of the state's unwillingness to direct much capital into agriculture in a major effort to increase productivity, it became increasingly concerned instead with the size of its share in what output there was. Under the system of procurement introduced (and still largely in force) the peasants had to sell to the state—after taxation—about half of their grain production and more than half their cotton, oilseed and sugar at artificially low prices, fixed by the government as a form of indirect tax. Once the quotas had been fulfilled, the peasants could either consume or sell to the state what little they had left.

The government made a handsome profit by selling the procured commodities at home and abroad. To provide at least subsistence for everybody, after 1953 the government rationed grain and cotton throughout the country, and edible oil in the towns, by means of both coupons and price. Rations changed according to how much the government would or could make available. So-called luxury goods were rationed only by price, so as to absorb the surplus spending power of a rapidly expanding urban population. Government stocks, nevertheless, had to be released during 1956 and 1958 to stop inflationary pressures. During this period, the *per capita* standard of living dropped, except in the consumption of sweet potatoes and coarse grains. However, at the lower end of the social scale, many people enjoyed a sense of security and well being they had not had before.

By 1955 the economy was sorely out of balance. Industrial production and construction had been overplanned. Also much confusion and inefficiency had been caused by the numerous control figures specified by the ministries; supplies of raw materials were often delayed by the sheer weight of bureaucracy. But more important, industrial growth had been slowed down by difficulties in agriculture. Due to the poor harvest of 1953 the state's procurement targets had not been met. In 1954, when the harvest was poor again, the state procured too much grain and left the peasants in considerable difficulties. Thereupon Mao agreed with the 'crusaders' that production was unlikely to get worse while the state would most probably fare better, if the cautious policy of land reform and organizing peasants into mutual aid teams were now abandoned and the peasants collectivized. The subsequent launching of collectivization put an end to a three-year debate within the Party. But it took away the barriers of moderation which had kept the Party's enthusiasts under control for so many years. The good harvest of 1955 was followed by the first Leap Forward. Collectivization was carried out in one year instead of three. The result was a repetition of the sad experience of Russia and several other eastern European countries.

Livestock was slaughtered and the disruption caused contributed greatly to the poor harvest of 1956. Some back-tracking was essential. Collectives were disbanded in some provinces and free markets in foodstuffs reopened. To give the state a degree of certainty in planning, procurement levels were fixed in 1955 for three years in advance. If the harvest was good, the peasants were in luck; if it was poor, they had to make up the difference from their own supplies. While procurement figures were increased, the peasants were reconciled by higher government prices for agricultural products, whilst the prices of consumer goods were held fairly stable.

The social revolution that was carried out in agriculture was also pursued in industry and commerce under the Leap Forward of 1956. By 'redeeming' the capital of private enterprises at 5 per cent interest and converting the owners into salaried factory managers, the state removed the last private firms. What now remained, were state controlled 'joint enterprises'. As the government extended its control, it took away another element of flexibility from an economy already suffering from too much bureaucracy. Combined with this, the overtly ambitious targets of the Leap Forward caused so much waste and disruption that Chou En-lai, the prime minister, had to call a halt to the 'blind advance' in the autumn of 1956. And although by the end of the year the Party announced that the plan had been fulfilled a year ahead of schedule, China still had its back to the wall. A new approach was needed.

The Great Leap Forward and the Communes

China's efforts to industrialize along somewhat conventional Soviet lines clearly showed that agriculture—under the then current policies—could not produce the large surpluses required. The harvest of 1957 yielded only 1·3 per cent more than that of 1956 and so failed even to cover the increase in population. Over-population was becoming more and more serious; at over 2 per cent the annual increase in population was so great that it was also outstripping the demand for labour generated by the country's industrial expansion programme. Rural under-employment increased instead of declining. All this confirmed the crusaders' contention that the first plan had been too cautious. At the insistence of the crusaders the Party decided to step up the rate of output by 50 per cent during the second plan.

The new target, the Party admitted, would require twice as much investment as the first plan—which had taken up over twenty per cent of the national income—and despite increased productivity a commensurate squeeze on current consumption would be needed. Moreover, while China's financial resources were still so limited, the dual pressures of rapidly expanding population and high investment targets dictated a redirection of investment funds and a far more efficient use than in the past of existing plants and labour. Before the end of the plan it was widely recognized that China would have to curtail the luxury of having a large number of plants using expensive equipment. But the Party was unwilling to make a substantial shift away from heavy industries which needed large capital investments if they were to function at their best. Instead it stipulated merely that new plants should adopt the most labour intensive techniques suited to their line of production—even if the standard of output would thereby drop somewhat. The Chinese hoped that this would enable them to spread the available funds over more plants and so recover more quickly the money invested. Moreover, the Party considerably modified its approach to industrial organization—moving towards decentralization in the hope of getting greater flexibility and productivity in light industry.

In rural life too, the Party was faced with similar preoccupations. Two allied problems had to be met. One was to use fully the ever increasing pool of underemployed peasants without hastening the drift of population from the countryside to the overcrowded cities. Emphasis on labour-intensive light industry and handicrafts provided a partial solution. Another was found in directing the peasants to work on water conservancy and other construction projects. There still remained, of course, the old intractable problem of obtaining a surplus from agriculture large enough to cover both the minimum consumption needs of the rising population and the ambitious investment targets of the plan. The peasantry had to be organized so as to maximize their contribution to farm output as well as to non-agricultural production. To do this the Party entered an almost religious crusade to break down the barriers to China's modernization and sustained economic growth. The drive for a Great Leap Forward was soon to become institutionalized in the communes, in themselves a unique expression of the anti-professional outlook of the crusaders and of their faith in the power of the masses, once mobilized, to overcome all obstacles —an attitude that had been strengthened by the notable lack of enthusiasm for 'socialism' which the educated Chinese had displayed during the Hundred Flowers period of 1957.

The rural communes were set up in the summer of 1958 by merging collectives into huge units of some 20,000 people, whose lives were tightly controlled in every respect. The responsibility of the communes extended to light industry and construction projects as well as agricultural production. Nevertheless their prime objective was to provide greatly increased surpluses for the government. This was to be achieved partly by minimizing the peasants' consumption—if not through the hoped-for economies of scale (and control) of communal dining halls, then by cutting down individual rations. More important, output was to be raised by people making greater efforts under the campaign of the Great Leap Forward. Most important of all, the system of political pressures and of economic controls was developed to such an extent that it produced what may well enter the historical record as the greatest experiment in social engineering that the world has ever seen. The importance of individual material incentives was disastrously under-rated. The peasant's efforts were rewarded partly by the provision of free food in the communal dining halls and small amounts of clothing and other daily necessities as well. Also they were paid a small cash wage; however, this cash payment was not related to individual performance, but to the number of hours worked and the total output of the commune. The quality of a man's effort was largely ignored, and the reward distributed, without differentiation, to the efficient and the lazy alike. The peasants' private plots—which had provided most of their vegetables and vitamins and frequently between 20 and 30 per cent of their income—were taken over by the communes. All this resulted in discontent and declining productivity. The system was gradually dismantled under the pressure of successive calamitous harvests; bad weather accentuated the inherent weaknesses of the system and so speeded the collapse. By 1962 cash incentives were given to small production teams of about twenty families. The peasants were permitted once more to cultivate private plots and sell the produce in the free markets. The communal dining halls, which had proved unpopular and wasteful, were abandoned.

The difficulties encountered by the Great Leap Forward and the communal experiment were not by any means due entirely to organizational weaknesses. An inherent danger of the Great Leap Forward was the fact that it required so much emotional excitement and fanatical drive to get it under way that excesses inevitably followed. Too much was attempted with too little preparation. And the Party—which had invested so much of its prestige in the programme—was understandably slow to recognize and squash misguided ardour.

Local cadres had driven the peasantry too hard on all fronts. Indeed, the Central Committee of the Party eventually had to issue orders that the peasants were not to be worked more than twelve hours a day except in the busiest of agricultural seasons. Badly planned or wildly optimistic schemes for non-agricultural projects proliferated. Even the policy of using underemployed rural labour on construction and water conservancy projects— one of the principal concepts in the Great Leap Forward and one which scored impressive achievements—suffered from this. Much effort was wasted, and some real damage caused, by projects not being carefully planned. For instance, dams built on the higher reaches of rivers for irrigation sometimes let too little water flow into the irrigation channels on the lowlands. Again, much of the bumper grain crop of 1958 was wasted because too many peasants were engaged in non-agricultural projects at harvest time. Perhaps the most unrealistic, and certainly most spectacular, project of the Great Leap Forward was the decision to have the communes turn to backyard furnaces and small-scale mining after the harvest of 1958. A tremendous amount of human energy and raw materials were wasted, and could not avoid being wasted in this scheme. Nearly all of the projects of the backyard furnaces were virtually useless. Similarly the transport of coal from the new small mines to the industrial centres was not only prohibitively costly but also disrupted the country's transportation services and interfered with the flow of essential materials to the industrial centres. By 1960 the scheme was abandoned and the peasants once more focused their attention on agriculture.

Despite all this China made progress during the Great Leap Forward—even if considerably more modest than originally hoped for and claimed. Superb climatic conditions had blessed the country with a record harvest in 1958. This enabled China to buy more Soviet machinery and complete plants in 1959–60 than during previous years, while at the same time allowing construction work to proceed much faster than in 1957. The attempt to bring industry to the countryside at least provided an educational bonus, giving peasants their first contact with industry. At times this resulted in the discovery of unknown talent.

At the Crossroads

The Great Leap Forward and the Communes had been launched in 1958 with the hope that China would overtake Britain in terms of total industrial production within fifteen years. Within three years, however, China had been brought to the verge of economic collapse. Before the initial chaos of the Great Leap Forward and the Commune movements had been sorted out, China was plagued with three years of natural disasters. Russia's withdrawal of its technicians from China and its refusal to deliver a wide range of industrial equipment added to China's difficulties. There was a slump in both agricultural and industrial output.

Because so many powerful people in the Party had backed the policies of the Great Leap Forward and the Communes to the hilt, it was not until the beginning of 1961 that the Party called for a policy of 'readjustment'. Industrial development was cut back and attention focused on agriculture. The communes were reorganized until they were but pale shadows of the great hopes they once inspired. They were responsible for administration and organizing co-operation among the peasants who now worked in small teams, in much the same way as they had done before the communes came on the scene. Paid for what work they did in these small teams the peasants had much more incentive to work hard. Moreover, the peasants had been given back private plots of land.

Despite the shift in policy things still got worse; for many people life was exceedingly hard. Revolts broke out in Mao's home province of Hunan and in Sinkiang. For a short time no effort was made to control the border and more than 100,000 Chinese poured into Hong Kong. It was not until the end of 1963 that the Chinese felt that their economy was once more on an even keel, although no further forward. In the previous five years China's leaders had done much soul-searching.

They seem to have emerged with a much better understanding of China's problems and much more agreed about how they could tackle them.

Although China's new long-term economic plan may not be launched until 1966, when China hopes to have all debts to Russia paid off, the main lines of approach have already been sketched out. Priorities have been reversed and China's economic salvation is now thought to lie in the modernization of agriculture. The aim is that industry should support agriculture—with agricultural machinery, fertilizers, insecticides, and consumer goods to induce the peasants to work harder—so that increased production will give a surplus to invest in industry and agriculture. Even so, China's leaders are talking cautiously and sensibly in terms of the modernization and mechanization of agriculture taking twenty to twenty-five years.

Much more attention is now being paid to making people aware of the needs for efficiency and scientific experiments if China's economy is to be modernized. A new status has been given to the professional and managerial class in the hope that it will now give of its best. The attempt in the Great Leap Forward to make progress without them was a bitter failure. Expertise is much more respected than it was. If the Party can restrain those cadres who tend to dislike anything 'intellectual' from interfering with the experts, China's gain will be all the greater.

The communists seem at pains to show sympathy with the peasants while making them aware of the great problems that have to be faced. In agriculture the government is concentrating its funds on 'growth centres', in the hope of getting high returns on investment. Even in these 'growth centres' the emphasis is going to be on modernizing rather than mechanizing agriculture. Mechanical equipment and fertilizers are expensive and will be scarce for some years to come. Better irrigation (with the help of water pumps) and improved methods of cultivation can do much to boost crop yields. The communes seem to have settled down, with the small team as the main production unit in day-to-day work and the commune authorities organizing co-operation on such things as irrigation work.

In industry, planning has once more been centralized in the government ministries. The ministries are trying to improve the efficiency and quality of production. Industrial know-how is going to be acquired from abroad by importing the most up-to-date equipment. In the last six months of 1963 China ordered seven complete chemical plants costing more than £33 million. Most of the plants are expected to be working by the end of 1966.

China's new long-term approach to economic planning and growth has much to its credit. Whether or not the Chinese Communist Party will follow this policy through, or how successful it will be we do not know. Nevertheless, China's considerable achievements and tragic human failures have given the world plenty of issues to ponder.

NOTES

The following are the main works in English on this subject.

Wu Yuan-li, *An Economic Survey of Communist China*. New York 1956.

Li Choh-ming, *Economic Development of Communist China*. Berkeley 1959.

——Economic Development—The First Decade, *The China Quarterly*, 1 (January–March 1960).

——*The Statistical System of Communist China*. Berkeley 1962.

Hughes, T. J. and Luard D. E. T., *The Economic Development of Communist China 1949–60*. London 1961.

Luard, D. E. T., The Chinese Co-operative Farm, in St. Anthony's Papers, *Far Eastern Affairs* 2. London 1960.

——The Chinese Communes, in St. Anthony's Papers, *Far Eastern Affairs* 3. London 1963.

Some of the main Chinese works on this subject have been collected and translated in *Communist China 1955–1959: Policy Documents and Analysis* (Introduction by J. K. Fairbank and R. Bowie). Cambridge, Mass. 1962.

CHAPTER SIX

THE CONCEPT OF ECONOMIC GROWTH

RONALD HSIA

Economic growth, as envisaged by the Chinese communist leaders, is essentially a process of transforming a preponderantly agricultural society into a modern industrial economy with a high degree of self-sufficiency in basic industrial materials and manufactures. This transformation, which requires a top priority development of heavy industry, is, moreover, to be carried out as rapidly as possible through forced industrialization and socialization under overall planning. A high tempo is thus implied in China's growth concept and calls for a conspicuous emphasis on linkage effects, labour-intensity and non-material incentives. This paper examines the growth rate and how it affects the pattern of development.

Rate of Growth

The official statistics of Communist China present the economy's net domestic material product (NDMP)[1] in index form with 1952 as the base year and also in annual percentage increase. The data for the period 1953–1959 are given in columns 1 and 2 of Table I. During the seven-year period, the NDMP increased 1½-fold, yielding an annual average growth rate of 14 per cent.

This incredibly high rate is upward biased for the following reasons. First, the agricultural output in the base year is underestimated in official statistics.[2] Second, the 'new product effect' tends to be heightened in a rapidly industrializing economy which stresses heavy industry. Third, the agricultural as well as industrial output is grossly overestimated for the Leap Forward years of 1958 and 1959 when China Mainland statistics were manipulated to arouse the workers' enthusiasm and ended in a state of confusion.[3]

The extent to which the official statistics exaggerated the growth rate of the Chinese economy can be checked against the estimates of China's net domestic product for the same period made by Liu and Yeh.[4] The corresponding index numbers and annual increases derived from their estimates appear in columns 3 and 4 of Table I. On the basis of their estimated net domestic product, the annual average growth rate is 8·2 per cent for the period 1952–1959. This rate is comparable to the growth of the Soviet economy during 1928–1937,[5] although their estimates are not completely free from some of the growth-exaggerating factors mentioned above.

An average growth rate of 8·2 per cent per annum is, nevertheless, excessive for the Chinese economy in view of its limited investment resources. It could not have been achieved without a substantial lowering of living standards. Liu and Yeh's study reveals that as late as 1957, the *per capita* consumption on the Mainland was 11 per cent below the meagre level of 1933.[6]

The lowering of living standards was unavoidable because of the lopsided pattern of planned development. From the very beginning of the plan era, attention was focused on the rapid build-up of heavy industry. This policy demanded that the economy's investment resources be concentrated on heavy industry and thus made possible its spectacular rate of growth (see Table II). The latter, in turn, leavened the growth rate of the economy as a whole (compare columns 2 and 4 of Table I with columns 4 and 5 of Table II).

The high tempo of forced development beyond the economy's capability resulted in the wide fluctuations of annual growth rate, as shown in columns 2 and 4 of Table I. These fluctuations during the seven-year period can be measured by the standard deviation of 9·8 for the official series. The large deviation may indicate that the annual average growth rate is too high and cannot be maintained with the available resources of the economy,

TABLE I

INDICES OF CHINA'S NET NATIONAL PRODUCT
1953–1959
(on the basis of 1952 prices)

YEARS	NET DOMESTIC MATERIAL PRODUCT		NET DOMESTIC PRODUCT	
	INDEX (1952 = 100)	ANNUAL INCREASE (PER CENT)	INDEX^a (1952 = 100)	ANNUAL INCREASE (PER CENT)
	(1)	(2)	(3)	(4)
1953	114·0	14·0	105·5	5·5
1954	120·4	5·7	111·0	5·2
1955	128·3	6·5	115·2	3·8
1956	146·3	14·0	128·9	11·9
1957	153·0	4·6	133·5	3·5
1958	205·0	34·0	151·6	13·6
1959	249·3^b	21·6	174·4	15·0

^{a} Derived from value estimates. ^{b} From annual percentage increase.

SOURCES: State Bureau of Statistics, *Wei-ta ti shih-nien* (Ten great years), Peking 1959: 18; *Jen-min Jih-pao*, 23 January 1960; Ta-chung Liu and Kung-chia Yeh, *The Economy of the Chinese Mainland; National Income and Economic Development, 1933–1959*, Princeton 1963, pp. 213 and 661.

TABLE II

INVESTMENT AND GROWTH OF HEAVY INDUSTRY
1952–1959

YEARS	RATIO OF INVESTMENT OF HEAVY INDUSTRY TO OVERALL INVESTMENT (PER CENT)	RATIO OF INVESTMENT OF HEAVY TO LIGHT INDUSTRY	INCREASE IN INVESTMENT IN HEAVY INDUSTRY (PER CENT)	GROWTH OF HEAVY INDUSTRY	
				GROSS VALUE OUTPUT (PER CENT)	NET VALUE OUTPUT (PER CENT)
	(1)	(2)	(3)	(4)	(5)
1952	29·4	3·2	—	—	—
1953	29·3	4·7	82·8	36·5	26·5
1954	34·8	4·7	35·0	19·8	18·6
1955	40·5	7·1	19·3	14·5	17·6
1956	39·7	6·2	56·0	40·0	45·0
1957	44·4	5·6	4·4	18·4	12·1
1958	56·6	6·9	46·3	103·0	28·2
1959	n.a.	n.a.	n.a.	43·3	32·0

SOURCES: State Bureau of Statistics, *Wei-ta ti shih-nien* (Ten great years), Peking 1959: 48 and 52; Liu and Yeh, *op. cit.*; Ronald Hsia, 'Les caractéristiques du développement industriel de la Chine continentale', *Tiers-Monde*, 2(7), Jul.–Sept. 1961: 338.

given the institutional framework and production organization. Significantly, drastic institutional and organizational changes took place in the years registering excessive rates of growth. The turbulence of such radical changes, however, introduced strong disequilibrating forces which pushed the economy into a state of imbalance.

Acute shortages developed in the supply of special steels, copper, timber and coal, whereas the supply of pig iron, ordinary rolled steel and cement was in excess of demand. The high rate of industrial growth, plus the enlarged scale of capital construction, caused great difficulties in the transport sector. The expansion of manufactures outstripped the development of raw materials resulting in the low rate of capital utilization in most of the consumer goods industries.[7]

Mao's Concept of 'Balanced Growth'

To justify such imbalances and to maintain the high rate of growth, Mao Tse-tung formulated a new concept of 'balanced growth', according to which, any balance is temporary and conditional, relative rather than absolute. In his celebrated speech 'On the correct handling of contradictions among the people', delivered at the enlarged session of the Supreme State Conference in February 1957, Mao said:

By 'balance' we mean a temporary, relative unity of opposites. By the end of each year, such a balance, taken as a whole, is upset by the struggle of opposites, the unity achieved undergoes a change, balance becomes imbalance, unity becomes disunity, and once again it is necessary to work out a balance and unity for the next year. This is the superior quality of our planned economy.[8]

This relativity concept of 'balanced growth' was a few months later elaborated on by Liu Shao-ch'i[9] as to the way in which a temporary, conditional balance between the various sectors of the economy is to be attained. According to Liu, such a balance should be brought about by pushing ahead the sectors that have lagged behind rather than pulling in the advanced sectors, so that the balance would be on a higher physical plane. In this way, the process of economic growth becomes a constant 'rat race' at a maximum tempo.

Steel as the Leading Link

Mao's concept of 'balanced growth' with its keynote on imbalance leads logically to exploiting linkage effects, both forward and backward.[10] Since the steel industry has the greatest total linkage,[11] it is not at all surprising that the communist leadership in China chose steel as the leading link in its Great Leap Forward. The linkage effects of the steel industry were emphasized by Wang Ho-shou, Minister of Metallurgical Industry, in these words: ' . . . a high rate of growth of the steel industry does not end in the steel industry itself; its speedy development inevitably gives an impetus to an accelerated growth of the other industries, transport and communications . . . a high rate of growth of the steel industry is bound to speed up social construction as a whole'.[12] The steel industry thus became the leading sector to which all other industries were unequivocably subservient in the allocation of materials, labour and transport facilities, and was expected to pull and push ahead all related industries.

The significant role of the steel industry in a developing economy is well known. It was all the more important to the Chinese economy at that juncture because of the sudden call for iron and steel for farm implements demanded by the agricultural plan, for water conservancy construction, and for the new-type local means of transport.[13] Moreover, the three million-odd rural factories established in the first part of 1958 (and the 26,000 people's communes formed subsequently) also led to an acute shortage of iron and steel.

Consequently the policy of 'steel as the leading link', in the high tide of the Great Leap Forward, produced a nation-wide fanatic mass movement having for its slogan 'the entire nation making steel'. Backyard furnaces mushroomed, and millions of

people all over the country took part in their construction and
the production of iron and steel. Two million crude iron-
smelting furnaces were built or rebuilt in the latter part of
1958.[14] Ironically, this development, aggravated by the linkage
effect, proved detrimental to the economy.

Labour Instead of Capital

The determination of the communist leaders to achieve a
high rate of economic growth was handicapped by the factor
endowment of the economy. Given the overwhelming abund-
ance of labour, economic growth is likely to be accelerated by
its full mobilization. Hence labour-intensive methods were
used from 1949 onwards in the formation of social overhead
capital,[15] and subsequently in agriculture, industry and other
sectors.

There is, however, a narrow limit within which labour can be
a substitute for capital, depending on the rigidity of factor
proportions in the production techniques used. Usually in
the technically advanced sector, the labour-capital coefficient
tends to be more or less fixed, leaving little room for raising
labour-intensity.

The communist drive to speed up economic growth in the
second plan quinquennium, therefore, led to opening up an
enormous 'new' production front where labour intensity can be
substantially increased by adopting indigenous production
techniques and reducing the scale of operation. Thus, in
agriculture, labour-intensive techniques such as deep ploughing,
close planting and painstaking weeding were promoted. Similarly, the industrial sector started a frantic movement to build
small-scale, labour-intensive producing units.[16]

This intensive use of labour called for institutional changes
to mobilize it on an enormous scale, thus leading to the
communization movement. In the latter part of 1958, some
26,000 people's communes emerged in the rural areas, and
involved over 99 per cent of the nation's peasant households.

On the average, each commune contained 4,637 households at the end of 1958.[17] In conjunction with the regimented communal life and the release of the female labour force from domestic work, it shows to what extent the rural communes were used in mobilizing and organizing labour for capital construction, agricultural production and industrial pursuits.

Non-material Incentives

The importance of labour incentives in economic development lies in the prospect of increasing labour productivity at a given level of capital investment. Such an increase can be expected from a greater exertion of labour and/or innovations of the type which require little additional capital input. Realizing the indispensability of labour incentives in an over-populated, capital-poor economy, Peking has resorted to various 'incentive' measures, both material[18] and non-material, with chief emphasis on non-material incentives so as to reap the increase in marginal product at zero marginal social cost. This is consistent with a high rate of investment for rapid economic growth.

Among non-material inducements are prestige awards such as the title of labour hero, the distinction of a special merit certificate or a red banner, the offer of Communist Party membership, and the honour of seeing Mao Tse-tung. These measures enhance the morale of the workers by giving public recognition of their achievements, and are without material cost to the economy.

Another measure is a series of emulation campaigns designed to elicit additional productive efforts by appealing to the competitive spirit. Once the workers' spirit is aroused, it drives them to extreme physical and mental exertion, and promotes team work. It has been used chiefly in the fulfilment or overfulfilment of production plans. To some extent it has served to raise economic-technical targets, such as the emulation campaign launched in the spring of 1959 to improve the utilization coefficient of the nation's big modern blast furnaces. The increasing importance of this measure is also seen in its gradual extension from within a plant to between plants, and from regional to nation-wide emulation.

A third measure is to apply mass movements to economic planning and production. Essentially this tends to arouse a sense of participation, inspire ingenuity in innovation, and play upon group psychology which commands personal sacrifices, as evidenced in pledges workers made at mass meetings either for setting exceptionally high targets, or for overfulfilling the predetermined tasks. Given the level of investment, such pledges could only be honoured by raising labour productivity through greater efforts, and, possibly, through improved working methods.

Concluding Remarks

The enthusiasm and overconfidence of the communist leaders, particularly from 1958 onwards, prompted them to seek an excessively high rate of growth with little regard to economic factors and in this pursuit they ran down the reserves of the economy to a dangerously low level. Since the open-end planning system requires unduly large reserves for fulfilling top-priority tasks, they imposed added strain and rigidity on the economy. Despite their ingenuity in exploiting non-material incentives and linkage effects, and their intensive utilization of labour, the growth rate rose in only two years, 1958 and 1959 (see columns 2 and 4 of Table I). In 1960, with food crops dropping to the 1957 level, the net national product declined, in spite of a reported 18·5 per cent increase in gross industrial value output.[19] The 1960 rate of growth has been estimated to be −4 per cent.[20]

While the poor performance of the agricultural sector was attributable to both human and natural factors, the adverse effects of the industrial leap forward cannot be overestimated. The nation-wide campaign for building small industrial units, notably the backyard furnaces and the mass participation in their production, plus the increased labour-intensity in other sectors, led to a labour shortage especially in agricultural production. Moreover, it put an additional strain on transport so that some of the agricultural output could not be transported as scheduled.

The prolonged agricultural crisis, in turn, affected the industrial sector in various ways. First, it led to the reduction of the grain rations of the industrial worker in September 1960, thus damping his morale and productive efforts. Second, it accentuated the shortage of raw materials for light industry. Third, it compelled Peking to use the country's precious foreign exchange (particularly in view of the dwindling export earnings) to purchase grains instead of capital equipment. Finally, it made necessary the transfer of labour from industry back to agriculture; by the beginning of 1961, some 20 million workers had been transferred back.[21]

Thus, at the Ninth Plenary Session of the Eighth Central Committee of the Chinese Communist Party held in January 1961, it was decided to reduce the 1961 scale of capital construction in heavy industry and focus attention on agriculture. This policy of top priority for agriculture and scaling down in industry was reaffirmed in September 1962 at the Tenth Plenary Session of the Eighth CCP Central Committee, and led to a wholesale close-down of factories, a return of private initiative in agriculture, and the development of selected industries servicing agriculture.[22]

A sense of economic realism now replaces the earlier ebullient optimism of the communist leaders, which brought chaos to the economy. Now that the crisis is over, China's economic growth will, perhaps, be guided by economic realism, less spectacular but better rooted.

NOTES

[1] The net domestic material product represents the aggregate value added by all the materially productive sectors minus depreciation. It differs from the Western concept of net domestic product notably in its exclusion of non-material sectors.

² For details, see Ta-chung Liu and Kung-chia Yeh, 'Preliminary estimates of the national income of the Chinese Mainland, 1952–59', *The American Economic Review*, **51** (May 1961): 490–92.

³ For a detailed account of the confusion in statistics, see Choh-ming Li, *The Statistical System of Communist China*, Berkeley 1962: Chapters VII and VIII.

⁴ As an approximation, the conceptional difference can be overlooked.

⁵ The average rate of increase in the net national product of the Soviet Union during 1928–1937 (the period covering the first two Five-Year Plans) computed on the basis of 1926/27 prices came to 8·0–8·8 per cent per annum. See Naum Jasny, *The Soviet Economy during the Plan Era*, Palo Alto 1951.

⁶ Liu and Yeh, *op. cit.*: 494.

⁷ *Rate of Capacity Utilization during 1957* (per cent)

Textile	85	Flour milling	68
Edible oil	75	Sugar refining	66
Leather	69	Cigarette	55

See Ronald Hsia, 'Growth capability of the Chinese economy as envisaged in the proposed Second Five-Year Plan', *Contemporary China*, **2** (1958): 63. Hong Kong University Press, Hong Kong.

⁸ *Jen-min Jih-pao* (People's Daily), 19 June 1957.

⁹ In his report at the Second Session of the Eighth National Congress of the Chinese Communist Party on 5 May 1958.

¹⁰ Forward linkage effects have the tendency to push ahead subsequent stages of production; backward linkage effects tend to pull up the activity level at the preceding stages of production. See Albert O. Hirschman, *The Strategy of Economic Development*, New Haven 1959: 98–104.

¹¹ *Ibid.*, p. 107. An examination of the steel row and column of the input-output matrix of an industrial economy will reveal the total linkage of the steel industry.

¹² *Hui-huang ti shih-nien* (Ten glorious years), Hong Kong 1959: 113.

¹³ An example of the new-type transport is a cart with ball-bearing axles.

¹⁴ *Chi-hua ching-chi* (Planned economy), Peking, No. 12 (1958): 21. The number of furnaces cited is undoubtedly a cumulative figure, in view of the extremely short life span of such furnaces.

¹⁵ The notable examples are water conservancy work, railway and highway construction. For details, see Ronald Hsia, *The Role of Labour-Intensive Investment Projects in China's Capital Formation*. Massachusetts Institute of Technology Cambridge, 1954.

¹⁶ About this, see Ronald Hsia, 'China's industrial leap forward' in *Symposium on Economic and Social Problems of the Far East*: 39–40. Hong Kong University Press, Hong Kong 1962.

¹⁷ *Wei-ta ti shih-nien* (Ten great years), Peking, 1959, p. 36. The number of rural people's communes has subsequently been increased to 74,000.

[18] Material inducements take the form of wage differentials, special monetary rewards, rewards in kind and social welfare provisions. The wage policy of the communist régime has been following the principle of wage rates according to skills and wage payments according to labour performed.

[19] Ronald Hsia, 'China's industrial leap forward' in *Symposium on Economic and Social Problems of the Far East*, Hong Kong 1962: 4.

[20] Yuan-li Wu, 'An interpretation of the industrial cutback in Communist China', *Current Scene*, **1**, (9): 2.

[21] *Hung-ch'i* (Red Flag), (1 February 1961): 26.

[22] In the midst of industrial cutbacks, for instance, the output of chemical fertilizers showed a 50 per cent increase in 1962. *Hung-ch'i* (23 Jan. 1963): 15.

CHAPTER SEVEN

THE PATTERN OF COMMUNIST CHINA'S AGRICULTURAL POLICY

WERNER KLATT

The failure of communist society to solve the problems of its village communities is a phenomenon deserving more than just a cursory mention. From the Bolshevik Revolution of 1917 to Fidel Castro's introduction of collective farming in Cuba forty-five years later, there has not been a single instance of agriculture flourishing in a communist state.* China is no exception in this respect. This phenomenon is all the more significant since communist régimes, though not as successful as they often claim, have had marked success in other spheres, such as in the rate of development in basic industries and the output of producer goods.

The apparent discrepancy between the performance of agriculture and that of industry is worth special examination, all the more because communism, contrary to earlier expectations, has failed to gain power in the industrialized countries of Western Europe which, according to Marxist doctrine, were to be the first to be led by the *avant-garde* of the industrial proletariat to revolution and progress. In fact, it has succeeded in seizing power only in countries predominantly agrarian in structure, underdeveloped in their economic and social infrastructure, and backward in their industrial make-up. All the more reason, one might think, not only to industrialize these countries, but at the same time to modernize their farming, still the largest single industry even in a country as industrialized as Soviet Russia.

Yet, in each instance, agriculture under communism has been a failure. It has not been merely a matter of a bad harvest

* In Poland and Yugoslavia, where most collectives have been dissolved, farming has done better than elsewhere in the Soviet bloc.

here and there; failure has been the general rule from which occasional success stands out as the exception. As a Yugoslav Professor of Farm Economics once put it sarcastically at an international conference in India: 'It is remarkable how the incidence of natural disaster increases with the forced collectivization of the land'.[1] The Professor spoke from deep insight into Yugoslavia's experience before and during collectivization as well as after it had been abandoned in his country.

China conforms to the pattern of communist failure in agriculture, but it would be an oversimplification to suggest that all that has occurred in the Chinese countryside (since the communist régime of Mao Tse-tung seized power in 1949) has been nothing but a repetition of what happened before in Russia or Eastern Europe, or more recently in Cuba. The pattern of agrarian structure and the mode of agricultural production differ too much from country to country to allow generalizations. Even in industry, which operates without undue dependence on conditions of soil and climate, generalizations must be subject to the proviso of 'everything else being equal'.

Since in agriculture conditions are rarely the same in any two places, it requires a special analysis of the main features of Chinese agriculture and communist attempts at correcting them, to isolate the specific elements of wisdom or error, and to assess the measure of success or failure that resulted,

Unsatisfactory Land Tenure

China is not only the country with the largest territory and the largest population in the world, she also has the largest number of villagers and farmers. As statistical documentation is scanty and of doubtful reliability even in times following a census—such as the first post-revolution census of 1953—all figures must be taken with a grain of salt. However, orders of magnitude are telling enough. At the time of the census, China's total population was said to be close on 600 million, with well over 100 million families (or 500 million individuals) living in more than half a million villages. As handicraftsmen, merchants, millers and the like live and operate in villages, the number of families engaged in agriculture proper might have been at that time approximately 100 million, equal to almost 250 million grown-ups working the land.

Where figures are so large and so imprecise, only rough approximations are possible in measuring the more subtle phenomena of village society, such as the extent of landlordism, owner-occupiership or land tenure. Even if communist data differ, for understandable reasons, from those of pre-revolutionary days, there can be no doubt that the conditions on the land left much to be desired in the years preceding the revolution. Again orders of magnitude must suffice: more than half the land under cultivation was owned by less than one-tenth of the farm population. At the other end of the social scale two-thirds of the farm population had to make do with less than one-fifth of the land cultivated. The social structure of the village society was thus marked by an extreme degree of polarization which was bound to cause discontent and to lead eventually to political explosion; all the more as the rents took up to 60 per cent of the gross product and interest rates on short-term loans amounted to 30 per cent and more per annum.

The steps taken by the Kuomintang and its leader Chiang Kai-shek to reduce rents by 25 per cent and interest rates to 20 per cent per year were inadequate, and Mao Tse-tung was preaching to the converted when in 1936 he coined, as the general line of his policy of nation-wide penetration, the slogan: 'Whoever wins the support of the peasants will win China; and whoever solves the land question will win the peasants'.[2]

As Mao and his closest followers confessed to being Marxists and communists, even if some of them did not have any of their training in the Soviet Union, the sequence of events following Mao's political pronouncements might have been anticipated. In fact, in a remote enclave of China, communist policy had been demonstrated in a Chinese Soviet Republic as early as 1927, and land legislation promulgated in Hunan gave, to those who visited the area, an indication of things to come.

After Mao had consolidated his position in the Party against Li Li-san, who had accepted uncritically the Soviet concept of the supremacy of the industrial proletariat in any future revolution, it became clear that a variant of the communist dogma was being introduced in China which was bound to result in revolutionary solutions different from those known from Lenin's seizure of power. Mistakenly more than one Western observer drew the conclusion that what was happening in China was a form of populist reformism and that it had nothing in common with the communist experiment as carried out in the Soviet Union.

Communist Agrarian Solutions

The history of China's agrarian policy has been recorded more than once[3] and need not be repeated here in detail, but its main features must be recalled lest the failure that followed early reform measures may not be understood fully. The principal elements of the agrarian programme of the Chinese Communist Party were laid down as early as 1927, when the significance of the peasants as a vital factor in any revolutionary development was registered for the first time in a resolution of the Party. The first test came in the early 'thirties' when policy statements had to be translated into day-to-day action in the Chinese Soviet Republic, which was inhabited very largely by cultivators. This practical experience, gained almost two decades before the application of the Party's policy on a nation-wide scale, proved invaluable.

There followed a time of tactical retreat during the period of the united front with the Kuomintang formed after Japan's invasion of the Mainland. Land reform measures were restricted largely to cuts in rents and interest rates, and they were thus almost indistinguishable from the policy adopted by Chiang Kai-shek. In the face of foreign invasion the policy of land distribution, which had been applied in the communist-held territory in 1931, was abandoned during the temporary truce with the class enemy. The period following the defeat of Japan

and the end of the Second World War was marked by vacilla-
tions in agrarian policy, ranging from the immediate confiscation
of landlords' property and its redistribution among landless
tenants and labourers in the north of the country to considerable moderation when the communists moved into territory in
South China that had previously been firmly in the hands of the
Kuomintang. A nation-wide land policy was introduced only
when the agrarian reform law was promulgated in June 1950.
By then the communist régime had established itself firmly
throughout the mainland of China.

As the reform measures that followed are well known in all
essentials,[4] they will be recalled only in brief outline. It is
an account of initial success followed by disaster on a vast scale.
Mao had once expressed himself in favour of 'a little terror'.[5]
In fact, much cruelty accompanied the reform. It was
carried out in four stages: in the first phase the villagers were
to be roused to action. Where discontent was not vocal, it was
to be created. 'Struggle meetings' were organized at which landlords were identified, accused, often beaten up and sometimes
executed on the spot. This frequently preceded the second
phase during which the class status of all villagers was to be
determined. Thereafter, during the third phase land and
property were confiscated, without compensation, and redistributed. In the final phase old title deeds were destroyed and
new landholding certificates issued.

In the course of the reform nearly 125 million acres were
taken from some four million large owners and redistributed to
nearly 50 million smallholders, landless peasants and farm
labourers. Thus, at the expense of 4 per cent of the farming
community, the status of half the village population was raised
from that of poor peasants and labourers to that of middle
peasants. Equally, if not more important was the classification
which formed the basis of confiscation and redistribution. The
grouping was as crude as the statistics on which it rested. Yet it
served its purpose of dividing the village against itself. Wrong
classification might mean death (at the top of the scale) or at

least exclusion from land distribution (at the middle layer). Landlords tried to prove that they were rich peasants; rich peasants that they were middle peasants; and middle peasants that they were poor peasants. Confusion and demoralization must have reached stupendous proportions. In the outcome, the poor half of the rural community raised to the status of middle peasants became, for the first time in generations, the proud holders of land and title-deeds, expecting to be in control, from now onwards, of output and disposal of crops and animal produce.

The magnitude of the debacle that followed can only be grasped if this phase of communist agrarian policy is understood in its full significance. Where the landlord is annihilated, the state always has to take over his functions, i.e. to collect and sell the surplus, to impose the levies and to provide credit. These functions did not fall unexpectedly upon the communist authorities. In fact, Liu Shao-ch'i, the Party's theoretician, had anticipated them when he spoke in June 1950 to the National Committee of the Chinese People's Consultative Council. Explaining the reasons for the agrarian reform law he said: 'The basic aim of agrarian reform is not purely one of relieving peasants. It is designed to set free the rural productive forces from the shackles of the feudal landownership system of the landlord class so as to develop agricultural production and thus pave the way for New China's industrialization'.[6]

Collectives and Communes

The ultimate target was thus obvious, and close adherence to the Soviet model of collectivization could be expected. There had been protestations to the contrary, e.g. in 1952 Kao Kang, the powerful head of the North East region, had insisted that the Chinese version of mutual aid teams and 'co-operatives' was based on the principle of private ownership and thus not comparable with the Soviet type of collectives which administered publicly-owned land. There were other voices, such as that of a member of the Party's Central Committee who warned that peasants cannot be controlled directly by the state. In the outcome, the transformation from individual to collective farming followed the Soviet precedent. The constitution which foreshadowed this development provided for the creation of producers' co-operatives, the forerunners of the collectives. These were introduced, contrary to all expectations, as early as 1955 after Mao's statement on 'co-operatization of agriculture'. By the end of 1957 the process of collectivization was completed except in some remote hill areas.

The Chinese cultivator's hope, raised in the early stages of the revolution, that he would be allowed the free disposal of his own produce was shattered within a few years. When the deliveries of grain proved insufficient to meet the requirements of the rapidly increasing industrial population, China followed the road of the Soviet Communist Party, intensifying the complusory collection of farm products by way of the collectives, instead of setting up an exchange, mutually advantageous to town dwellers and villagers, of farm requisites for foodstuffs. Thus ended the short period of success in communist agrarian policy and of rural co-operation with a Party, which was set on rapid industrialization at the expense of the countryside and therefore bound to get into conflict with the nation's chief productive operator—the cultivator.

Soon it became clear that the collectives brought no solution of the Party's unsolved problems in the countryside. Before the cultivators had had time to get fully accustomed to this innovation, yet another experiment was introduced in the villages. The communes created in the summer of 1958 produced conditions even grimmer than what the Russian *kulak* had had to endure thirty years earlier. When the Party recognized during the brief period of the Hundred Flowers that it could count as little on the support of the intellectuals as on that of the cultivators, it decided to try a momentous experiment in social engineering. The mass of the population was to be housed, fed and educated in barracks and to be directed from there to communal work on farms, on roadsides and industrial establishments set up for the occasion. The re-educated, reorganized Chinese masses were to fill the gap created by the inability of Soviet Russia, preoccupied with restoring order in Eastern Europe, to aid China's second Five-Year Plan.

From the summer of 1958 to the end of the year some 750,000 collectives were amalgamated in 26,000 communes. Whilst the collectives had supervised on average some 150 families, each of the communes was made responsible for some 5,000. More than 100,000 peasant families were supposed to have abandoned within six months a way of life which had been an integral part of China's tradition for centuries. Whereas the responsibility of the collective had usually covered the territory of a village, the area of control allocated to the commune was eventually extended to an average of three country districts. So large an area would have been an unmanageable administrative unit, even if the Party cadres in charge of the operation had been more qualified than in fact they were.

There was no lack of zeal on the part of the cadres. When it was proclaimed as the Party's target to double production in agriculture and industry within twelve months, many if not most units did not dare to report anything but fulfilment of the target set. Thus was allegedly made the so-called Great Leap Forward, a political and economic enterprise without precedent. At the same time values and loyalties that had prevailed in China for centuries were discarded in one gigantic sweep. The anticlimax which was bound to follow was of equally momentous dimensions.

Setbacks in Farming and Food Supplies

In the sphere of agricultural production, the chief claim for 1958 had been raised from 196 million tons of grain planned to 375 million tons allegedly harvested, an increase of 100 per cent within twelve months. The exaggeration was on so vast a scale that most Western observers felt unable even to guess its magnitude. When most of the grain had been consumed, the harvest claim was eventually revised to 250 million tons. In fact, 220 million tons seems to be the most that is likely to have been gathered. The exaggeration, which had formed part of the attempt to reduce rural society within a few months to complete submission, had been exposed before the new harvest could be gathered. The year 1959 brought the end of the Great Leap Forward. Thereafter the communes continued to exist in name rather than in reality. The chief responsibility for output and delivery of farm products reverted rapidly to the village as the natural administrative unit.

Other concessions were to follow, but not before three years of harvest failures had brought hardship to the nation as a whole and had caused malnutrition among many consumers in the food deficit areas, particularly at the end of the crop season. It is not easy to come by facts in this matter since Chinese sources were careful to keep silent about the extent of hardship caused by the errors committed by Government and Party. Western observers were divided among themselves about a situation which was unprecedented. Few were permitted to get close to the reality of life in China in the years following the Great Leap Forward, and those who did were not necessarily the best judges of the situation. At the height of success some were deceived as 'nothing convinces more than success'; others spoke at the depth of failure of 'the downward spiral', as if China had not been for centuries at the mercy of the extremes inflicted by Nature and man, and the Chinese had not lived through many ups and downs.

When all available information, such as official statements and refugee reports as well as nutrition surveys made in China and in Hong Kong is taken into account and expressed in internationally recognized units, it appears that the average national consumption fell from the exceptionally high level of 2,200 calories per head per day in 1957 to 1,850 calories and less in 1959–1961. As the privileged must have consumed considerably more, this implies cases of malnutrition, of one form or another, in deficit areas, particularly at the end of each of the three crucial consumption years. To alleviate the situation, China changed from exporting some grains and soybeans, as was done up to 1958, to importing wheat and wheat flour at the rate of approximately 5 million tons a year from 1960 onwards. While the Canadian and Australian grain saved China from worse disaster, it contributed no more than 50 calories a day to the average diet of the Chinese nation or, expressed differently, it did little more than provide for the additional requirements of the growing population. In fact, the grain was of course shipped mainly to the largest urban and industrial consuming areas north of the Yangtze river.

Even before the calamities of the early sixties, the Chinese diet, grossly overburdened with carbohydrates, had been deficient in sugar, vegetable fats, animal proteins and vitamins, and signs of malnutrition could be seen even in 'normal' years. When the calorie intake fell to 1,850 calories and less, this did not lead to the state of nation-wide starvation which some Western students of Chinese affairs had predicted.[7] It did nevertheless have serious consequences.

It is not always understood that man can be brought to a state of nutritional equilibrium at a reduced level of energy intake, well below his habitual consumption. Nutrition surveys during and after the last war revealed in Europe as well as in Asia that man can live on a low plane of nutrition for substantial periods, without necessarily suffering any serious physical damage or indeed becoming unduly susceptible to illness or disease. Food satisfies basal metabolism, maintenance requirements and energy needs for work. Shortage of food thus means in many cases a decline in work rather than incidence of malnutrition. This is the meaning of Chinese official instructions in 1960 to extend the hours of rest of the working population.

Under Chinese conditions, an average food intake of 2,200 calories per day is likely to provide the population with ample food for heavy work. At the level of 2,000 calories the population will remain in reasonably good physical condition. Below that level there is bound to be loss of body weight, retarded growth among children and reduced output among working men and women. All these defects were observed in 1960. In such circumstances cases of malnutrition were bound to occur in areas badly supplied with foodstuffs, particularly at the end of the seasons 1960–61 and 1961–62. Even more serious than the incidence of malnutrition was the drastic decline in the output of workers, both in rural and urban areas. This is likely to have had its repercussions well beyond the years of nutritional deficiencies.

Revised Farm Policies

In spite of the seriousness of the situation, the Party was slow in revising its farm policy in other than administrative respects. In fact, the over-ambitious twelve-year agricultural programme of 1956 was endorsed, without any serious amendments, by the National People's Congress as late as the spring of 1960.[8] This programme, covering the period from 1956 to 1967, was conceived early in 1956, a few months after the first Five-Year Plan (1953–57) had been published belatedly. At that time long-term planning was being considered throughout the Soviet orbit as an alternative to planning for periods of five years only. The Chinese agricultural programme was designed as a master plan for the period terminating with the end of the third Five-Year Plan. It represented, however, little more than an expression of intent. The targets set for 1967 were over-ambitious and unrealistic.

The optimism displayed by the authors of the programme rested on the erroneous assumption that accumulated gains could be derived from a programme of various improvements, the success of each of which in fact depended on the simultaneous application of modern methods in several spheres. Irrigation and flood control ranked highest on the list of measures to be taken, and as distribution canals and ditches had been neglected badly during the years of war and civil war, considerable improvements were indeed possible. Other measures such as mechanization, seed multiplication, pest and disease control, land reclamation, multiple cropping and the application of fertilizers could be expected to contribute modestly to increases in yield, if they were applied side by side with one another.

As it stood, however, the programme lacked co-ordination and integration. As it began to be implemented, it revealed its principal weakness, an appalling lack of funds. Less than one-tenth of all public investment was set aside for agriculture, water conservancy and forestry together, and two-thirds of this small amount was devoted to water conservation and irrigation. Thus yields remained in essence dependent on the hazards of Nature the impact of which was not softened, in spite of all official manifestations to the contrary, by any introduction of farm requisites such as fertilizers or mechanical draught power.

As the prospects of progress varied with the change in the weather and the controversy vacillated between rightist and leftist elements in the Party, so the twelve-year agricultural programme suffered its downward and upward changes. An abridged version was issued in the autumn of 1958 when the campaign in favour of merging collectives into communes was at its height. It was allegedly drawn up by Mao Tse-tung himself as a charter for agriculture. In the report to the National People's Congress it was described as even richer and more complete in content than the agricultural programme. Its chief innovation was the inclusion of 'close planting' as one way of achieving increased yields. This method was abused so much in 1958 that it was exposed to serious criticism by farm specialists, later branded as 'rightists'. Little has been heard of it in recent years.

The harvest failures of 1959 to 1961 were due as much to human failings as to the hazards of Nature which, however, were blamed exclusively in the official accounts. Only slowly did it dawn on Government and Party that an end had to be put to the adventures of the last few years and that remedies had to be found to meet long-term needs. The first remedial measures were in the nature of makeshifts. Although questions of farm management had been transferred from the communes to the so-called production brigades, the communes remained the ultimate institutional aim, the current system being regarded merely as a temporary expedient. There were other expedients, modelled on the pattern known from the period of Lenin's New Economic Policy. In particular, the cultivators were encouraged to supplement the output of the public sector by sideline production from the small family-plot which had once again become permissible. The same applied to private trade in the products of the family plots, principally vegetables, eggs and poultry. Last, but not least, bonuses in kind were re-introduced so as to spur the members of production brigades (village communities) and production teams (family units) to additional efforts.

In the meantime the inner-Party controversy between rightists and leftists continued, but by the time the National People's Congress met early in 1962, the moderates seemed to have gained a partial victory over the extremists. While China's relations with Russia and the non-communist world continued to be dictated by doctrinal rigidity and revolutionary zeal, economic policy at home was guided by a 'revisionist' attitude of considerable, if temporary, moderation. Contrary to all previous procedure, farming was given pride of place in economic planning and investment policy, to be followed by light and heavy industries in that order. Priorities, as they had existed in China for a decade and in Soviet Russia for a quarter of a century, were thus reversed. No information has been released, though, on industrial or agricultural targets or on the allocation of budgetary resources to investment and working capital in the various sectors of the economy. It is therefore impossible to gauge the extent to which priorities were in fact altered. What is certain, however, is the salutary effect which the change has had. The year 1963 brought the first tangible improvements, in five fateful years, to the national economy.

The statement, issued at the end of the year when the National People's Congress met, again failed to reveal any data on the degree of fulfilment of the plan. It seems fairly certain, however, that the harvest was a little better than in any of the previous three years. Even if it surpassed slightly the harvest of 1957, it failed to provide the population, which had meanwhile grown by the equivalent of that of Great Britain, with a food supply *per capita* equal to the not very ample amount available in the last year before the Great Leap Forward.

It was therefore not surprising to learn that the order of economic priorities introduced early in 1962 was to continue beyond the end of 1963. Nevertheless, the National People's Congress, probably in deference to critics of this 'revisionist' policy, emphasized that while 'agriculture was the foundation of the economy, industry was the guiding principle'. Even if this appeared to be no more than a re-statement of previous Party political declarations, the emphasis seemed to have shifted somewhat in favour of industry. In any event, no doubt was left about the temporary nature of the current order of priorities. As soon as conditions permit, the countryside may well be sacrificed once again in the interest of speedy industrialization.

Economic Balance Sheet

Where farm policy is so much a matter of temporary expediency, a balance sheet of past achievements and failures and of economic prospects in the foreseeable future is bound to be tentative and open to revision.[9] What is certain is that agriculture, which is still the largest and most important sector of China's economy, will remain so for a long time to come. Its failure is all the more serious. In the last decade it has shown little, if any, improvement in volume or quality of output, and its contribution to the nation's total product has declined in relation to other spheres of economic activity. It has had to carry, nevertheless, most of the burden of the industrialization programme, and as matters stand, this will again be the case after a brief period of temporary reprieve. Whereas Nature has been blamed exclusively for the misfortune of three consecutive poor harvests, it has been due mainly to man's failings that the rate of growth in farming has not even kept pace with the natural increase in population. The shortfalls in farm output have resulted more than once in the maldistribution of food, in cases of nutritional deficiency, if not malnutrition, and in grave loss of work capacity among labourers in town and country.

The effects of the agricultural policy on the development of industry may be even more serious and more lasting than in agriculture itself. The process of 'primitive accumulation'— without which economic progress is impossible as in capitalist society—has been upset greatly and, as a result, industrialization has been slowed down severely and the national income has hardly increased as much as the population whose living standard has experienced none of the promised improvement. It is in fact more likely to have declined. As economic and technical assistance from the Soviet Union, China's only donor of aid, seems to have come virtually to a standstill, the process of industrialization depends now entirely on the progress made in agriculture. In the course of the first decade of its life, Communist China moved a long way towards industrialization, but it is still a long way off becoming an industrial nation.

In 1960, the last year for which reliable Chinese figures are available, industrial countries such as Japan, Soviet Russia, Britain and the United States produced respectively eight, ten, seventeen and almost twenty times as much steel per head of population as China. This set of data may serve as a measure of the long road that China has yet to travel and of the big contribution which its farming population will have to make before the economic ambitions of its leadership are within reach of fulfilment. Before this comes about, Nature may distribute bountiful harvests in some years but may impose hardship in others. The modernization will not advance fast enough to eliminate the hazards of the weather.

In the meantime, unless substantial amounts of foreign capital come to China's aid, a series of good harvests may well tempt the communist leadership to start another reversal of priorities. A small, if not a great leap forward, may once again become the overriding object of economic policy. In the course of the first fifteen years of its rule the Communist Party of China has shown a deep understanding of the use of revolutionary tactics not only during the stage of popular reforms, but also during periods of unpopular measures, such as the introduction of collectives and communes. It is likely to repeat these tactics when it decides to enforce once again its doctrinal principles in the face of popular opposition.

That China's farming industry has failed is obvious and, in this respect, China is not unique among communist countries, all of which have had similar experiences. The question remains why this should be so. Without going into detail on the doctrinal errors that underlie communist agrarian policy and that are ultimately responsible for the continuous lack of success of its agricultural planning and performance, a few essential points may be singled out.[10]

Conclusions

Although Mao and his political lieutenants have been much closer than the Soviet and East European communist leaders to the problems of the villages, they have always considered industrialization as the only true form of communist society and agriculture as the chief source of revenue with which to finance the industrial development of the country. Therefore from the very beginning of their rule they sought to extract a maximum of deliveries from the villagers with which not only to feed the growing urban and industrial population, but also to pay for the equipment required by industry. As a corollary of this policy, agriculture has been starved consistently of capital investment, its essential means of modernization. In a political climate of this kind the intensification of farming, keeping in step with a moderate degree of industrialization, could not be expected. Over-hasty industrialization and neglect of farming led of necessity to the larger and ever larger units of the collectives and communes, through which the Party hoped to extract the levies, which it had been denied as long as the close-knit village communities remained intact.

When this policy failed to yield results, the villagers were allowed control over strictly limited plots of land and portions of the market. Whilst this dualism of public and private sectors of production and marketing unquestionably has had a favourable effect on the farming community, it holds at the same time the seeds of its own destruction. Contrary to what happens in industry, in agriculture the producer is at the same time to a large extent a consumer of his own produce. This results in a relationship between producer and produce which differs radically from that of the industrial worker. The existence, side by side, of public and private markets and of low official delivery prices and high prices in the open markets opens the way to large-scale diversion of farm labour and agricultural produce from controlled channels into uncontrollable ones. The communes with their mess halls were an attempt to overcome this shortcoming. They did not succeed.

What the Chinese communist leadership failed to grasp, in spite of its former close association with life in the villages, was the fact that agriculture, though following basically the principles of other human activities, has certain characteristics which one ignores only at one's peril. To mention only the most obvious differences: whereas in industry most operations can take place within a strictly confined space without being affected by the vagaries of natural conditions, farmers have to take into account weather and space as the chief limiting factors of all their operations. Communists once in power, being orientated towards urban life and industrial pursuits, have always ignored the special characteristics of agriculture and have blamed the cultivators whenever their approach to farming met with failure. This has led to an antagonism, for which there seems to be no remedy, between the communist rulers and the villagers they rule—and that means in China some four-fifths of the population.

However, the worst mistake of all lies in the erroneous concept of which all Marxists and communists have been victims. They invariably regard small-scale farming as economically backward and the small-scale cultivator as politically reactionary and hostile towards the industrial working class. With this assessment they have caused an implacable antagonism which has bedevilled communists in and out of power all over the world. Whilst the communist type of industrialization, though different in its aims from that of its non-communist counterpart, does not vary altogether in its structure and in its approach to problems of advance, communist agrarian policy is an attempt not merely to break with the past, but to act against all precedents. It thus flies in the face of all historical experience.

Instead of concerning themselves with the problems of capital-intensive farming in a growing industrial community, communists continue to waste their time on the outmoded question of the optimum size of farming. The theoretical misunderstanding and the only limited doctrinal flexibility in the face of a never ending series of failures have created a dilemma that the Chinese communist leadership seems unable to escape. The political leaders and economic planners of newly emergent countries will wish to study carefully this phenomenon before deciding on their own course of action.

NOTES

[1] Andrew Shonfield, 'The Poona Conference of Economists', in *The Observer*, London, 29 February 1961.

[2] Mao Tse-tung, *Selected Works*, Vol. I: 32. London 1955.

[3] Chao Kuo-chün, *Agrarian Policy of the Chinese Communist Party, 1921–1959*. London 1960.

[4] W. Klatt (1961), 'Chinese Agriculture as a Model for Asian Countries', in *Symposium on Economic and Social Problems of the Far East*, edited by E. F. Szczepanik. Hong Kong 1963.

[5] Mao Tse-tung, *Selected Works*, Vol. I: 39. London 1954.

[6] Liu Shao-ch'i, *The Agrarian Reform Law*. Peking 1950.

[7] W. K., 'The state of nutrition in China', in *The China Quarterly*, 7 (July–September 1961).

[8] W. K., 'Communist China's agricultural calamities', in *The China Quarterly*, 6 (April–June 1961).

[9] W. Klatt, 'The economy of Communist China', in *Asia*, London 1965.

[10] W. K., 'Soviet agriculture as a model for Asian countries', in *The China Quarterly*, 5 (January–March 1961).

TABLES

TABLE I
LAND REFORM

a. STATUS OF FARMERS BEFORE LAND REFORM

FORMS OF TENANCY	1928[1]	1929–1933[2]	1935[3]
	IN PER CENT OF TOTAL HOUSEHOLDS		
Landowners	51·7	54·0	46·0
Tenants	26·2	17·3	30·0
Part Tenants	22·1	28·7	24·0
	100·0	100·0	100·0

b. POPULATION AFFECTED BY LAND REFORM

FORMS OF HABITATION	1950	1951	1952
	IN MILLIONS		
Rural Population	145	290	385
Total Population (in rural areas)	160	340	450

c. CONFISCATION AND DISTRIBUTION OF LAND

REFORM MEASURES	HOUSEHOLDS	FARM AREA	AVERAGE FARM SIZE
	MILLIONS	MILLION ACRES	ACRES
Confiscation	4	120	30·0
Distribution	50	120	2·4

d. STATUS OF FARMERS BEFORE AND AFTER LAND REFORM

FARMERS' CLASSIFICATION	1928[4]	1949[5]	1955[6]
	IN PER CENT OF TOTAL HOUSEHOLDS		
Landlords	14·7	4·0	—
Rich Peasants	16·2	6·0	10·0
Middle Peasants	24·7	20·0	70·0
Poor Peasants	44·4	70·0	20·0
Total:	100·0	100·0	100·0

Sources:

[1] L. L. Chang (1930), in *The China Critic*, Shanghai.
[2] L. Buck (1937), *Land Utilization in China*, Shanghai and Chicago.
[3] National Agricultural Research Bureau (1938). *A Statistical Analysis of Tenancy in China.*
[4] *Hankow Land Commission Report*, 1928.
[5] Ching I-hung (1950). *China's Land Reform and China's Land Problem*, Hong Kong.
[6] *The Economic System of Chinese Society*, Peking 1955.
[b] Various Official Chinese Communist Statements.
[c] Various Official Chinese Communist Statements.

TABLE II

COLLECTIVIZATION

a. FARM ORGANIZATION

TYPES OF ORGANIZATION	1950	1953	1956	1959	1962	1963
	ORGANIZATIONS IN 000					
Mutual Aid Teams	2,700	7,450	n.a.	—	—	—
Agricultural Co-operatives						
lower level	negl.	15	682	—	—	—
higher level	—	negl.	312	negl.	—	—
total	negl.	15	994	negl.	—	—
People's Communes	—	—	—	24	n.a.	74

b. ORGANIZED FARM HOUSEHOLDS

TYPES OF ORGANIZATION	1950	1953	1956	1959	1962	1963
	HOUSEHOLDS IN MILLIONS					
Mutual Aid Teams	11·3	45·6	n.a.	—	—	—
Agricultural Co-operatives						
lower level	negl.	0·3	10·4	—	—	—
higher level	—	negl.	107·4	negl.	—	—
total	negl.	0·3	117·8	negl.	—	—
People's Communes	—	—	—	122·0	(124·0)	n.a.
Private farms	94·2	70·4	2·2	1·2	(1·0)	n.a.
Total:	105·5	116·3	120·0	123·2	(125·0)	n.a.

TABLE II *(Continued)*

COLLECTIVIZATION

c. AGRICULTURAL PRODUCTION AND LIVESTOCK

CROPS AND LIVESTOCK	1949 ACTUAL	1952 ACTUAL	1957 ACTUAL	1959 CLAIM	1960 CLAIM	1962 TARGET
Crops (million hectares)						
Grains and Potatoes	101·6	112·3	120·9	121·3	(120·0)	n.a.
Soybeans	8·2	11·5	12·6	12·8	(13·0)	n.a.
Cotton	0·3	0·5	0·6	0·6	(0·6)	n.a.
Crops (million tons)						
Grains and Potatoes	108·0	154·5	185·0	270·5	297·0	250·0
Soybeans	5·1	9·5	10·0	11·5	12·5	12·5
Cotton	0·4	1·3	1·6	2·3	2·5	2·4
Livestock (millions)						
Horses, Donkeys and Mules	15·8	19·6	19·8	(20·0)	na.	n.a.
Cattle and Buffaloes	43·9	56·6	65·8	(65·4)	n.a.	90·0
Pigs	57·8	89·8	145·9	(180·0)	(243·0)	250·0
Sheep and Goats	42·3	61·8	98·6	(112·5)	n.a.	170·0

d. AGRICULTURE DURING GREAT LEAP FORWARD

CROPS AND LIVESTOCK	1958			1959		
	TARGET ORIG.	CLAIM ORIG.	CLAIM FINAL	TARGET ORIG.	TARGET REV.	CLAIM FINAL
Crops (million tons)						
Grains and Potatoes	196·0	375·0	250·0	525·0	275·0	270·0
Soybeans	10·4	12·5	10·5	15·0	15·0	11·5
Cotton	1·7	3·3	2·1	5·0	2·3	2·4
Livestock (millions)						
Pigs	180·0	200·0	160·0	280·0	180·0	n.a.

Sources: Various Official Chinese Communist Statements.

TABLE III
FOOD SUPPLIES
a. FOOD RATIONS. 1960–61

FOODS	PER MONTH		PER ANNUM	
	LIGHT WORKERS	HEAVY WORKERS	LIGHT WORKERS	HEAVY WORKERS
Grains	25 lb.	40 lb.	135·00 kilos	218·00 kilos
Sugar	4 oz.	4 oz.	1·35 kilos	1·35 kilos
Meat	12 oz.	12 oz.	4·10 kilos	4·10 kilos
Vegetable oils	12 oz.	12 oz.	4·10 kilos	4·10 kilos

b. GRAIN IMPORTS. 1960–63

COUNTRY OF ORIGIN		1960/61	1961/62	1962/63	1960/61–1962/63
		MILLION TONS			
Canada					
Wheat and flour		1·60	2·00	0·90	4·50
Other grains		0·60	0·20	—	0·80
	Total	2·20	2·20	0·90	5·30
Australia					
Wheat and flour		1·85	0·60	3·25	5·70
Other grains		0·40	0·05	—	0·45
	Total	2·25	0·65	3·25	6·15
Other Countries					
Wheat and flour		—	0·80	—	0·80
Other grains		0·35	0·95	0·25	1·55
	Total	0·35	1·75	0·25	2·35
		US$ MILLIONS			
Canada		130	155	65	350
Australia		120	40	190	350
Other Countries		30	85	15	130
	Total	280	280	270	830

c. ESTIMATED FOOD CONSUMPTION

FOODS	1960/61		1963/64	
	KILOS PER HEAD	CALORIES PER DAY	KILOS PER HEAD	CALORIES PER DAY
Grains (inc. Potatoes)	183·0	1,550	185·0	1,575
Pulses and Soybeans	10·0	100	10·0	100
Sugar	3·0	30	2·5	25
Fruit and Vegetables	60·0	50	80·0	70
Meat and Poultry	8·0	65	10·0	70
Eggs and Fish	6·0	15	7·5	20
Fats and Oils	4·0	90	4·0	90
Total	274·0	1,900	299·0	1,950

Sources: Official Chinese Sources, International Trade Statistics, Estimates.

CHAPTER EIGHT

SINO-SOVIET ECONOMIC RELATIONS: CHINESE DEPENDENCE ON SOVIET AID

WERNER KLATT

The break between China and Russia seems inescapable. Even if the Soviet leaders do not insist on the excommunication of Communist China and relations are not broken off formally, the damage done to China seems irreparable. This is particularly true of the setback which the Chinese economy has suffered and continues to suffer. The dislocations caused by an over-ambitious programme of industrialization, which went under the name of the Great Leap Forward, and were followed by a series of poor harvests, were aggravated by the withdrawal —allegedly without any forewarning—of Soviet economic and technical assistance. Industrial plants which had hardly started operating had to be closed; large-scale projects which formed an integral part of the second Five-Year Plan were abandoned; men and women returned to the villages which they had left only recently in search of work; the nation's physical and human resources had to be reallocated, and political, economic and social priorities rearranged. This led to an all-round stagnation. The country will take many years to recover from this setback.

Conflict and Disruption

It would be wrong to see Sino-Soviet relations and their disruption exclusively in economic terms. The friction is on a much wider front and the schism started long before economic relations became strained.

To all appearances, the split was caused by a disagreement over 'peaceful coexistence' and over liberation from colonial rule by revolution. In fact, the reasons for the struggle raging since 1958 are much more complex. Only at the end of 1962 did the depth of the disagreement come into the open when Peking and Moscow began referring to each other by name instead of criticizing Yugoslav revisionists and Albanian dogmatists. Thereafter even an observer, untrained in communist semantics, could no longer be in doubt about the seriousness and dimensions of the conflict.

The current dispute may well end in a schism. There is something ecclesiastical about the atmosphere in which the struggle is fought and proselytes are sought. Not unlike the schism of the eleventh century it started with what the non-believer might have regarded as trivialities. It led unavoidably to mutual recrimination and condemnation when vital national interests were at stake.

The deep gulf between the Orthodox Eastern and the Catholic Western wings of the Christian Church, which had been dug by Pope and Patriarch, remained unbridged even in the face of the advancing enemy. Even if the historical parallel must not be drawn too far, it may serve as a reminder to both Peking and Moscow that relations can be formally maintained, although ideological reconciliation may be out of the question. This state of affairs has indeed existed for some years. Formal relations have been maintained in spite of the strain caused by the political controversy. In the future, as in the past, this state of affairs may well continue. In the final analysis, communists probably hate and fear the infidels even more than each other.

China's communist leaders are unlikely to forget how much they have suffered as a result of their dependence—ever since the early twenties—on the Soviet Union. After they had seized power in 1949, this painful dependence emerged as an inescapable feature of China's very existence. Having few, if any, friends in the world and little political intercourse with non-communist powers, China had to leave much of her diplomatic representation to the Soviet Government. When pursuing her national interests in Korea and Formosa, she had to ask for Soviet military equipment; worse still, when she got involved in an armed conflict with her chief Asian rival, India, she found Soviet Union sitting on the fence and eventually supplying air cover to her enemy.

Last, but not least, the size of China's industrialization programme and the pace at which it was carried out, was largely dependent on the volume and composition of the economic contribution which the Soviet Union was willing to make. Soviet consent was even more essential when China engaged in a programme of economic and political probing in territories beyond her southern borders.Here a clash of interests was brought into the open in 1955, when Khrushchev toured South and South East Asia.

Isolated and weak, China had but one effective weapon of her own: to challenge Soviet supremacy in the arena of world communism. She did so when, after the Hungarian revolt of 1956, she saw that she would not be able to count on Soviet assistance to the extent required in the implementation of her second Five-Year Plan. China's claim, in 1958, that the communes provided the means by which she would reach the communist millennium ahead of the others, was a direct challenge to Soviet leadership in the ideological sphere. The doctrinal struggle thus became *inter alia* an expression of frustrated economic ambition.

Contradictory Statements

It would be wrong to suggest that Sino-Soviet relations have been one continuous disappointment to China and the main, or indeed the only, cause of political friction between China and Russia. Although Soviet aid has been small, Sino-Soviet trade (imports and exports combined) increased, within a decade after 1949, from less than $500 million to more than $2,000 million. During these years several thousand Soviet technicians helped in the erection of almost 200 industrial plants.

During this period and even after the withdrawal of Soviet technical assistance, relations between the two powers were as often cordial as cool. When a Soviet delegation led by a deputy minister of foreign trade arrived in Peking as late as February 1961 to hold talks on questions of mutual assistance and economic co-operation, China's foreign minister praised the eternal, unbreakable brotherly friendship and the monolithic solidarity between the two countries. Marshal Ch'en Yi also praised the tremendous help received from the Soviet Union and promised to remain forever grateful for this assistance.

Other statements markedly different in tone and contents were made at about the same time. Chou En-lai, when asked by Edgar Snow whether the Soviet Union had given any aid without compensation, said: 'Generally speaking, no; but in a specific sense, one can say, yes'; but he made no reference to capital equipment or technical expertise. Relations were clearly strained. When Sino-Soviet trade was heading towards an all-time record, Soviet assistance was described as unprecedented in history (*People's Daily*, 14 February 1959); but on the whole the emphasis was on self-reliance rather than on foreign aid. This has been the general theme in public pronouncements since the inauguration of the second Five-Year Plan. Peking radio summarized the sentiments of the Chinese communist leadership (5 May 1957) in these words: 'China should never rely on foreign aid for socialist industrialization'.

These conflicting accounts of Sino-Soviet economic relations show the ambivalence in the ever-changing relations between the two countries. The frequent contradictions found in official Chinese pronouncements make it difficult for a Western observer to bring order into the record of Sino-Soviet economic interdependence and to interpret it intelligibly.

Record of Sino-Soviet Economic Relations

Apart from one minor case of grant-in-aid offered on the occasion of Khrushchev's visit to Peking in the autumn of

1954, Soviet economic assistance to China has consisted of long-term financial aid, technical assistance and expanded trade. As to its magnitude, there remains some doubt. Soviet aid, although small in comparison with China's needs and Soviet assistance to communist Eastern Europe or non-communist India, has made an important contribution to China's post-war recovery and industrial development.

Soviet credits have played only a small role. The exact amount of long-term loans has been under dispute for some time, but it is now generally accepted that China has had only two credits for non-military use:

(a) a sum of $300 million, granted in February 1950 at 1 per cent interest per annum, paid in five annual instalments of $60 million each, repayable at the rate of $30 million a year from the end of 1954 to 1963; *(b)* a credit equivalent of $130 million granted in October 1953 at 2 per cent interest per annum, other terms not having been divulged.

Nothing is known of the size of the Soviet Union's contribution to China's armed intervention in Korea nor terms under which it was granted. Unofficial estimates made at various times range from $500 million to $1,000 million; it is thus difficult to assess with certainty the position of China's balance of payments. Her relative liquidity in recent years would imply that the repayment of her military debt does not present insurmountable problems. Official Soviet and Chinese statements on the subject of financial aid throw no light on the situation; they have on the contrary added to a state of confusion, which cannot have helped China to raise loans outside the Soviet bloc.

In 1957, after the fortieth anniversary of the October Revolution the Soviet Union stated that its aid to countries within the communist camp totalled some 28,000 million roubles or $7,700 million at the official rate of exchange (*Izvestia*, 18 October 1957). Li Hsien-nien, the minister of finance, in his budget report of June 1957 stated that the Soviet Union had extended to China economic assistance amounting to nearly 5,300 million *yüan*, or approximately the same amount in roubles at the exchange rate apparently operating in Sino-Soviet transactions. (There is some reason to doubt whether this rate of exchange was in fact applied.) At the official rate in force at the time this sum was equal to $1,325 million.

This sum, while excluding charges for the Soviet Union's return to China of the Changchun Railway and the harbour of Port Arthur, included the Soviet share in the joint-stock companies, if not the value of some fifty Manchurian plants first dismantled and then restored to China. But large amounts remain unexplained since the two long-term loans of 1950 and 1954 amounted to little more than 1,700 million roubles. Some observers have concluded that large consignments of military aid granted during and after the Korean war, or short-term debts on trading account, must have increased China's indebtedness to the Soviet Union. Others have dismissed Soviet claims of large-scale assistance as empty shows, because the agreements of mutual assistance of April 1956 and February 1959 excluded the possibility of long-term credits and imposed repayment out of current production, supplied under cover of annual trade protocols. The truth may never be known.

Soviet Projects in China

The evaluation of Soviet technical assistance to China, like that of financial help, is fraught with difficulties. In 1956 the number of projects aided by Soviet equipment and technicians was stated to be 211, ranging in average cost of materials and technical assistance from the equivalent of $9·2 million per project in the early stages of development to $11·4 million per project in 1956. Later the 211 projects were amalgamated and their reduced number was 166. In August 1958 and February 1959 another 125 projects at average costs ranging from $11·7 million to $16 million each were added, bringing the number of projects to 291, the total cost to 15,300 million

TABLE I

SINO-SOVIET TRADE 1950–1963

a. SOVIET EXPORTS—CHINESE IMPORTS

YEARS	TOTAL 000 MILLION OLD ROUBLES	TOTAL $ MILLION	MACHINERY AND EQUIPMENT	IRON AND STEEL	MINERAL OIL AND OIL PRODUCTS	OTHERS
			PERCENTAGE OF TOTAL			
1950	1·55	387	10·6	5·2	2·9	81·3
1951	1·91	478	22·6	10·4	9·2	57·8
1952	2·22	554	28·1	12·0	5·8	54·1
1953	2·79	697	23·5	10·4	6·4	59·7
1954	3·04	759	26·2	11·6	5·9	56·3
1955	2·99	748	30·9	10·7	10·6	47·8
1956	2·93	733	41·6	8·5	11·7	38·2
1957	2·18	544	49·9	6·0	16·7	27·4
1958	2·54	634	50·1	9·6	13·5	26·8
1959	3·82	955	62·6	5·0	12·4	20·0
	MILLION NEW ROUBLES					
1960	735	817	61·7	7·2	13·9	17·2
1961	331	368	29·4	9·4	33·0	28·2
1962	210	233	11·9	11·9	34·3	41·9
1963	168	186	22·6	14·9	32·7	29·8

b. SOVIET IMPORTS—CHINESE EXPORTS

YEARS	TOTAL 000 MILLION OLD ROUBLES	TOTAL $ MILLION	FOODSTUFFS	INDUSTRIAL RAW MATERIALS	TEXTILES, CLOTHING, FOOTWEAR	OTHERS
			PERCENTAGE OF TOTAL			
1950	0·76	191	46·4	15·9	8·9	28·8
1951	1·32	331	32·9	18·9	10·2	38·0
1952	1·65	414	44·0	25·3	13·0	17·7
1953	1·90	475	44·4	25·0	15·8	14·8
1954	2·31	578	45·7	22·8	15·9	15·6
1955	2·57	643	43·3	22·7	18·3	15·7
1956	3·06	764	40·5	19·8	20·0	19·7
1957	2·95	738	29·5	22·0	21·3	27·2
1958	3·52	881	31·6	17·0	25·2	26·2
1959	4·40	1,100	26·3	14·0	40·5	19·2
	MILLION NEW ROUBLES					
1960	763	848	19·7	14·5	46·5	19·3
1961	496	551	3·1	16·0	58·9	22·0
1962	465	516	7·2	12·4	60·6	19·8
1963	372	413	5·2	11·4	65·5	18·0

(old) roubles or $3,825 million and the average cost per plant to $13 million. According to the open letter of the Central Committee of the Communist Party of the Soviet Union (*Pravda*, 14 July 1963): 'with the active assistance of the Soviet Union, People's China has built 198 enterprises, shops and other projects equipped with up-to-date machinery'. Thus well over 100 plants, or one-third of those projected, never passed the planning stage. Soviet supplies and assistance are likely to have been of the order of $2,500 million. This may or may not include the value of Soviet know-how and expertise as well as the training of Chinese students and technicians in Russia.

This form of Soviet assistance has been reflected in Sino-Soviet trade transactions and in the short-term debts which China was allowed to accumulate in the course of this trade. Here the record of Sino-Soviet economic relations is very much less ambiguous than other parts, although even there some uncertainty remains. It is, for instance, doubtful whether Soviet supplies of military equipment are included in the published foreign trade returns. Despite some uncertainties and resultant inaccuracies, the overall picture which emerges is highly revealing.

Chinese imports from the Soviet Union almost doubled between 1950 and 1954 to reach the figure of approximately $760 million, and they reached an all-time record of $955 million in 1959. In the short span of a decade the pattern of Soviet exports to China changed beyond recognition. The share of machinery and equipment increased from one-tenth in 1950 to almost two-thirds in 1959, when two-fifths of total trade consisted of complete plants. During this period China accumulated substantial short-term credits. Economic assistance is sometimes barely distinguishable from trade on deferred terms, and in fact Soviet trading practice allows for 'technical credits', i.e. swings which require payment of 2 per cent if they surpass agreed ceilings. China made extensive use of this provision. Trading balances to the amount of almost $1,000 million accrued between 1950 and 1955 in favour of the Soviet

TABLE II

a. SINO-SOVIET BALANCE OF TRADE 1950–1963

$ MILLION

YEARS	IMPORTS FROM RUSSIA	EXPORTS TO RUSSIA	TURNOVER	BALANCE
1950	387	191	578	− 196
1951	478	331	809	− 147
1952	554	414	968	− 140
1953	697	475	1,172	− 222
1954	759	578	1,337	− 181
1955	748	643	1,391	− 105
Sub-total	3,623	2,632	6,255	− 991
1956	733	764	1,497	+ 31
1957	544	738	1,282	+ 194
1958	634	881	1,515	+ 247
1959	955	1,100	2,055	+ 145
1960	817	848	1,665	+ 31
1961	368	551	919	+ 183
1962	233	516	749	+ 283
1963	186	413	599	+ 227
Sub-total	4,470	5,811	10,281	+1,341
Grand total	8,093	8,443	16,536	+ 350

Union. In 1956 China began to repay these and her trading deficit with the Soviet Union has by now disappeared. At the end of 1962 China could record a surplus of $125 million in her favour.

In the course of the thirteen years during which Sino-Soviet trade first expanded dramatically and later contracted with even greater vehemence, much Soviet equipment went to mining, fuel and power plants. An industrial base was thus laid on which China hoped to build her own self-sustained industrial economy. These expectations were shattered when doctrinal issues were allowed to interfere with economic development.

Before this happened, China received perhaps the most important form of assistance as a result of Soviet Russia's willingness to open her internal markets to Chinese consumer goods—a favour denied to most other trading partners of the

b. SOVIET CREDITS TO CHINA 1950–1965

$ MILLION

YEARS	DEVELOPMENT CREDITS	TRANSFER CREDITS (ESTIMATE)	MILITARY CREDITS (ESTIMATES)	TOTAL
Payments made:				
1950	60	—	400	460
1951	60	—	—	60
1952	60	—	335	395
1953	110	—	—	110
1954	110	—	—	110
1955	30	160	—	190
Grand total	430	160	735	1,325
Repayments due:				
1954	30	—	40	70
1955	30	—	40	70
1956	30	—	75	105
1957	30	—	75	105
1958	45	—	75	120
1959	45	25	75	145
1960	45	25	75	145
Sub-total	255	50	455	760
1961	45	25	75	145
1962	45	25	75	145
1963	45	25	75	145
1964	15	25	35	75
1965	25	10	20	55
Sub-total	175	110	280	565
Grand total	430	160	735	1,325

Soviet Union. The export of Chinese textiles increased from very modest beginnings to a value of over $350 million in 1959. When China ceased to be able to export agricultural surplus goods, textiles and clothing provided more than half of a greatly reduced export volume. In this way, more than in any other, China was able to repay the short-term trade credits which had accumulated in the early fifties.

TABLE III

a. SINO-SOVIET BALANCE OF ACCOUNTS 1955–1967

$ MILLION

	SOVIET CREDITS	REPAYMENT DUE		REPAYMENT MADE (TRADE BALANCE)	SURPLUS/DEFICIT ACCUMULATIVE	
		ANNUAL	ACCUM.		ANNUAL	TOTAL
Balance						
end 1955	1,325	—	1,580[a]	—	—	—1,580
1956	—	335[b]	1,245	31	—304	—1,549
1957	—	140	1,105	194	—250	—1,355
1958	—	150	955	247	—153	—1,108
1959	—	175	780	145	—183	— 963
1960	—	170	610	31	—322	— 932
Sub-total	1,325	970	610	648	—322	— 932
Balance						
end 1960	360[c]	—	970[d]	—	—	—970
1961	—	160	810	183	+ 23	—787
1962	—	164	646	283	+ 142	—504
1963	—	211	435	227	+ 158	(—277)
1964	—	216	219	(170)	(+ 112)	(—107)
1965	—	195	24	(107)	(+ 24)	0
Sub-total	360	946	24	(970)	(+ 24)	0
1966	—	12	12	—	—	0
1967	—	12	0	—	—	0
Sub-total	—	24	0	—	—	0
Grand Total	1,365[e]	970	0	(970)	—	0

[a] including interest rates and other costs, e.g. rouble cost of Soviet experts, but disregarding other charges, e.g. freight costs.

[b] including 195 due in 1954 and in 1955.

[c] including 320 funding of outstanding debts and 40 for sugar loan.

[d] including 360 as under *(c)* plus 610 due for repayment in 1961–1965.

[e] including 40 for sugar loan.

b. SOVIET CONTRIBUTIONS TO CHINA'S
ECONOMIC PROJECTS 1950–1963

$ MILLION

YEARS	NUMBER OF PROJECTS	VALUE OF SOVIET EQUIPMENT AND TECHNICAL AID		
		MILLION OLD ROUBLES TOTAL	$ MILLION TOTAL	$ MILLION PER PROJECT
Planned:				
1950 February	50 ⎫	5,200	1,300	9·2
1953 September	91 ⎬			
1954 October	15	400	100	6·9
1956 October	55	2,500	625	11·4
Sub-total	211	8,100	2,025	(Avg.) 9·6
Consolidated into:	166	8,100	2,025	12·2
1958 August	47	2,200	550	11·7
1959 February	78	5,000	1,250	16·0
Grand total	291	15,300	3,825	(Avg.) 13·1
Actual:				
1950–1963	198	10,000	2,500	(Avg.) 12·6

Mutually Advantageous Trading Pattern

Had China been free to choose her chief trading partners, she might have found others with more complementary economies and less prohibitive transport charges. Considering that she had little, if any, choice, a trade pattern developed which was of some mutual advantage, in fact more so than either side could have foreseen at the outset. As a result, China was able to speed up her industrialization. As Soviet Russia's share in China's foreign trade increased from a mere 5 per cent before the revolution to approximately 50 per cent in 1959, the Soviet Union became China's main foreign supplier. Russia's exports to China were at that time as large as those to all underdeveloped countries taken together. One-sixth of Russia's exports went to China; one-half of all Soviet exports of machinery and nearly three of every four complete plants sent abroad went to China. In the course of a decade the Soviet Union has supplied complete plants and factory equipment to the tune of well over $2,000 million. China for her part, at the height of Sino-Soviet commercial relations, rivalled East Germany as Russia's first trading partner, supplying twice as much to the Soviet Union as all underdeveloped countries taken together. China supplied one-fifth of Russia's total imports, two-thirds of her food imports and three-quarters of her textile imports.

Although no more than one-half of almost 300 industrial projects undertaken under cover of Sino-Soviet agreements had been completed by 1959, the Soviet Union had contributed substantially to China's take-off from agrarian backwardness to semi-industrial development. Within the decade beginning in 1949 China's share in the Soviet bloc's industrial potential had doubled from 5 to 10 per cent. The provision of thousands of Soviet specialists had not been the least important part of Russia's contribution. Their withdrawal marked the most painful phase of Sino-Soviet relations.

The first phase, up to the end of 1954, had been marked by extensive Soviet short-term credits coupled with some small long-term loans granted for non-military purposes and substantial, though unspecified, supplies of military equipment. At the same time the first steps had been taken towards technological and scientific co-operation between the Soviet Union and China, and the first major consignments of Soviet plant equipment and machinery worth more than $600 million had been delivered. Between 1955 and 1959, Soviet supplies of factory plants and other machines had almost trebled to more than $1,800 million, but China had paid out of current production not only for these goods but also for most of those received on short-term credit. The military aid and the value of the Soviet share of the joint-stock companies returned to China in 1953 are being repaid mainly in the form of Chinese agricultural raw materials and industrial consumer goods.

Strained Relations

Firm evidence of the strained relations came in March 1960 when negotiations regarding a long-term trade agreement were broken off, thus leaving China as the only country in the Sino-Soviet bloc whose trade was based on nothing more than an annual trade protocol. When this was signed, it showed the first planned reduction in the volume of Sino-Soviet trade. As this had been unexpectedly high, some decline might well have been in the interest of both trading partners, but other larger reductions were soon to follow. In the summer of 1960, following the first open Sino-Soviet dispute during a meeting of the Council of Mutual Economic Assistance in Bucharest, Soviet engineers, technicians and scientific advisers were abruptly withdrawn from China. This resulted in a sharp decline of Sino-Soviet trade, cancellation of some large-scale Soviet-aided projects and the general delay, if not abandonment of China's industrialization as envisaged in her second Five-Year Plan.

At the close of the Chinese National People's Congress in December 1963, the official Chinese press accused the Soviet Union of having brought pressure to bear on China, extending the ideological differences to the sphere of state relations; withdrawing almost 1,400 experts; tearing up some 340 contracts; cancelling over 250 items of scientific and technical co-operation; and reducing the supply of equipment, resulting in heavy losses to China's construction and dislocating its original development plan (*People's Daily*, 4 December, 1963).

Earlier in the year, the Soviet Union was also accused of having torn up in 1959 a defence agreement signed in October 1957, and of refusing to provide China with a sample of an atomic bomb and the technical data regarding its manufacture.

Notwithstanding these measures, Sino-Soviet trade relations were maintained, although the volume declined by one-fifth instead of one-twentieth as agreed in the trade protocol. As machines and mineral oil products continued to arrive in China, the question of a Soviet economic embargo may be dismissed, but commercial relations, though formally correct, steadily declined until they were reduced to a minimum of essentials.

These developments coincided with a series of very severe setbacks in China's domestic economy. Following the Great Leap Forward and the formation of the communes in the rural areas, farm production declined so drastically as to turn China from a minor food exporter into a major grain importer. The crisis, caused partly by nature and partly by man, necessitated an annual expenditure of some $300 million in foreign exchange for the purchase of some 5 million tons of grain in each of the consumption years 1960/61 to 1963/64. Whilst China had to turn to the West, the Soviet Union exported similarly large quantities of grain to Eastern Europe and beyond and extended her economic assistance at an increased rate to non-communist countries in the Middle East, to India and the Far East.

The bitterness of Chinese recriminations is understandable, for China had seen her interests sacrificed once before to those of the 'revisionists' in Eastern Europe and the 'national bourgeoisie' of Asia. In 1956–1957 when she was in the process of designing her second Five-Year Plan, the Soviet leaders, instead of offering China economic aid, were preoccupied, after the Hungarian revolt, with bringing order into Eastern Europe at the cost of almost $1,000 million in short-term credits. Little wonder that the Chinese felt incensed to find that rebellion yielded a better reward than loyalty. The poison which almost destroyed Sino-Soviet relations in recent years was probably laid in that fateful autumn of 1956.

The combination of internal and external difficulties deprived China in 1960 of the possibility of earning a trade surplus with which to repay her outstanding debts and she was granted a moratorium. The Sino-Soviet trade protocol of 1961 funded $320 million of outstanding commitments with the proviso that it had to be repaid by 1965. China drew the only possible conclusion from this state of affairs. At home, economic priorities were changed so as to secure the rehabilitation of the farming industry. Abroad, the emphasis was on an expansion of exports of consumer goods and a reduction of imports of capital goods. In this way China hopes to repay her debts by 1965 at an annual rate of approximately $200 million.

China began to repay her long-term debts to the Soviet Union in 1954 and she has used her trading balances for their repayment as well as those on current trading accounts. The size of her debts from invisible imports and other commitments is not known for certain, but her outstanding funded debt to the Soviet Union probably amounted in 1964 to no more than $200–250 million. At the present rate of repayment it is likely to be cleared well before the end of 1965. Thereafter, China will be able to concentrate on repaying the advances she has received from Western grain-producing countries and to send some of her export surpluses to markets where she can earn convertible currency.

Economic Retrenchment

A burden of this kind, coming on the top of heavy domestic commitments, made retrenchment in the industrialization programme inescapable. The revisions of original plans have been so drastic that it has apparently been considered inadvisable to publish plan results for 1960 to 1963 or the targets of the third Five-Year Plan which was due to start at the beginning of 1963. While the present economic priorities are likely to be maintained, at least until China has repaid her debt to the Soviet Union in 1965 (rather than in 1967, the nominal end of the third Five-Year Plan), the situation may become somewhat easier when China gathers her first satisfactory harvest since 1958 and can reduce her expenditure of foreign exchange on Canadian and Australian grain. In the meantime China is likely to transfer some of her external economic ties from the Soviet Union and Eastern Europe to Western Europe and Japan in an effort to regain some of the momentum lost in recent years in her industrialization programme.

Already in 1957, China began to expand her trade to countries in South East Asia and to turn to Western Europe for some of her industrial needs. Her present trade with non-communist countries, which accounts for over half the total, is largely determined by the necessity to pay for grain imports. As long as these cannot be reduced, imports of industrial equipment from Western Europe and Japan are likely to be strictly limited. Even if these imports become possible, the basically autarkic character of China's economy would hardly be affected. At present little more than 2 per cent of her total national product enters international trade. Only massive foreign aid, on the scale on which India has enjoyed it for several years past, could end China's present state of economic stagnation and political isolation. As matters stand at the moment, China is unlikely to find such assistance either within the Soviet bloc or outside it.

BIBLIOGRAPHY

Brzezinski, Z. K. *The Soviet Bloc, Unity and Conflict*. New York 1963.

Crankshaw, E. *The New Cold War, Moscow v. Peking*. London 1963.

Eckstein, A. 'Moscow-Peking Axis: the economic pattern' in *Moscow-Peking Axis* (H. L. Boorman *et al.*) New York 1957.

Floyd, D. *The Sino-Soviet Conflict*. London 1963.

Goldman, M. I. 'Sino-Soviet trade: a barometer', *Problems of Communism*, November–December, 1962.

Hoeffding, O. 'Sino-Soviet relations in recent years', in *Unity and Contradiction* (K. L. London) New York 1962.

——*Sino-Soviet Economic Relations 1958–62*. Rand Corporation, Santa Monica, Cal. 1963.

Hughes, T. J. and Luard, D. E. T. *The Economic Development of Communist China, 1949–1960*. London 1961.

W. K. 'Sino-Soviet economic relations', in *The Sino-Soviet Dispute* (G. F. Hudson *et al.*) London 1961.

Li, C. M. *Economic Development of Communist China*. Berkeley, Cal. 1959.

Li, C. M. *et al.* 'Chinese industry', *The China Quarterly*, Jan.–Mar., 1964.

London, K. L., ed. *Unity and Contradiction: Major Aspects of Sino-Soviet Relations*. New York 1962.

Szczepanik, E. F. 'Foreign trade of Mainland China', *Contemporary China*, Vol. III. Hong Kong University Press 1960.

——'Balance of payments of Mainland China', in *Symposium on Economic and Social Problems of the Far East*. Hong Kong University Press 1962.

Whiting, A. S. 'Contradictions in the Moscow-Peking Axis', *Journal of Politics*, February 1958.

——'Conflict resolution in the Sino-Soviet Alliance', in *Unity and Contradiction* (K. L. London) New York 1962.

Wu, Y. L. *An Economic Survey of Communist China*. New York 1956.

Zagoria, D. S. 'The future of Sino-Soviet Relations', *Asian Survey*, Apr. 1961.

——'The Sino-Soviet conflict and the West', *Foreign Affairs*, Oct. 1962.

——*The Sino-Soviet Conflict 1956-1961*. London 1962.

Part III

Politics taking Command:
A Political Assessment

CHAPTER NINE

THE INFLUENCE OF REVOLUTIONARY EXPERIENCE ON COMMUNIST CHINA'S FOREIGN OUTLOOK

A. M. HALPERN

The pattern of behaviour of any individual or group towards others is largely shaped in the course of day-to-day dealings. It often seems possible to analyse the behaviour of nations in terms of a bargaining process in which the material stakes on either side can be precisely calculated and the comparative advantages of alternative courses of action accurately estimated. In practice, however, one or both of the parties to a relationship define the situation in terms not solely of what an uninvolved third party sees as objectively present, but of intangible values, expectations and predispositions formed in other contexts of experience. The effect of such underlying attitudes varies from case to case and from party to party. It is never entirely negligible and never unchecked by realistic considerations.

The purpose of this chapter is to identify and describe some of the underlying attitudes of the mainland Chinese toward the rest of the world, not to analyse in full any specific instances of Chinese foreign policy in operation. In fact, we do not know enough about the Chinese people as a whole to accomplish this purpose; at best we can hope to describe some attitudes of the present régime, perhaps only of one segment of it, with no assurance that they are fully accepted by the mass of the population. The parts of its world view that the régime affirms most fervently, probably are exactly those the Chinese general public is least prepared to accept. If there were not independent evidence of the régime's attachment to these views, one would be inclined to evaluate them as propaganda and to discount the sincerity of even the top leaders' belief in them. The conduct of foreign policy seems to be little restricted by considerations of Chinese public opinion. Control of the means of communication is very nearly absolute. As long as the régime makes a plausible show of having a productive foreign policy, its views are likely to spread among the people and to become part of a common set of attitudes.

We can postulate that the context of experience in which the régime's basic orientation to the external world was formed was that which existed at the time the present top leaders were young men. All that we know of their personal histories indicate that they belong to the social-psychological type of the convert. They adopted communism as young men seeking certainty in an environment of social and political disintegration which offered no objective basis for it. They chose their ideology not as a result of cool reflection, but under the stress of a need to solve urgent personal problems. In such circumstances, the intellectual and emotional aspects of belief become inseparable, and the experience of defending beliefs by action further welds the two aspects together. This kind of conversion often has two characteristic features. First, the world view adopted is dualistic; it contains an absolute distinction between good and evil. Second, the convert feels an inner compulsion to convert others, even to the point of willingly accepting martyrdom as the price of failure.

Destruction of Traditional Authority

The situation against which the Chinese communists reacted was not altogether unique. For at least the last hundred years, the impact of the West on non-Western societies has produced comparable effects, in different degrees, wherever it occurred. Apart from the economic effects, there has usually been a degrading of traditional authority and of the system of shared values which made traditional patterns of social co-operation viable. The decline of traditional authority has quite commonly resulted in serious impairment of the ability of societies to distribute equitably those things their members value. This in turn has led to a failure of traditional processes of social control and a need for the construction of new control mechanisms. Such processes typically produce on the one hand new social groups of the go-between type, and on the other hand numbers of uprooted, frustrated individuals.

There is thus a basis for the Chinese communist belief that they share with all colonial and ex-colonial societies an important common experience, even though their claim is seriously overstated. In disintegrating traditional societies the individual's search for a solution to the problem of leading a satisfactory life is a vital necessity. The variety of possible solutions is rather wide. The choice made by the present leaders of Communist China was clearly an extremist one. In comparison with choices made by other Chinese or in other countries, it was the most thoroughly anti-authoritarian and morally uncompromising. Further, in contrast to many nationalist movements, the Chinese communist struggle was directed against both domestic and foreign adversaries. Under these conditions, the struggle assumed a form in which the primacy of political actions over all others was assured.

The Figure of Ah Q

The pre-revolutionary illnesses in Chinese behaviour against which the communists felt it necessary to struggle—by political means—are aptly summarized in the literary figure of Ah Q, created by Lu Hsün [Chou Shu-jen]. Mao Tse-tung himself has often expressed his admiration of Lu Hsün as a writer and of Ah Q as his most memorable character. As late as 1958, Chou Yang used Ah Q to point a moral in his address to the Asian and African Writers' Conference in Tashkent.[1] This figure, then, is that of an improverished, impotent, hopeless old man, constantly browbeaten and humiliated by events, who takes refuge from his inadequacies in fantasies of spiritual superiority, in which he identifies himself with his oppressors.

The Chinese communists rebelled against both the humiliation and the passivity of Ah Q's response. From the beginning of their adult lives their attitudes were strongly conditioned by consciousness of their national weakness, which they attributed in part to the hostility of foreign figures, in part to the ineffectiveness of traditional Chinese behaviour in coping with this hostility. The Soviet model of revolution recommended itself as having dealt with both sides of the problem. It was also sanctioned by an ideology according to which success was historically inevitable. Ah Q's fantasies were centred on identification with his oppressors; Mao identified with those who would destroy the oppressor. From the very beginning of the movement the dedication to activism and the emphasis on the necessity of struggle, which have been so prominent in recent Chinese ideological statements, were deeply ingrained.

With such a background, both friendly and hostile orientations tend to become emotionally supercharged. Wherever reality gives support to such predispositions, it reinforces them. It was to be expected that the Chinese communists would not only take note of the bipolar distribution of power after World War II as an actuality, but that they would regard it as fit and proper. Even though one discounts the more extreme examples of anti-American (or anti-imperialist) and pro-Soviet (or pro-communist) statements by the Chinese as due to tactical necessity—to reverse the residual pattern of preference of the Chinese public, or to promote some international bargaining process—the basic pattern of identification and antagonism is clear and deep-seated.

The Two Worlds

Sino-American conflicts over the past fifteen years have ranged from competition for prestige in third countries to armed conflict. Above and beyond these concrete occasions for enmity, the Chinese feel compelled to attribute American actions to a sort of virus of permanent hostility. Several observers have reported the deep-seated suspicion with which the

Chinese view every step the United States takes in a negotiation. Their reports give reason to suppose that Chinese statements analysing American motives as implacably hostile and aggressive are not made simply for tactical effect but reflect a real, almost an instinctive, distrust. The traditional American attitude toward the Chinese people, which still persists, is derived from missionary experience to an important extent. Missionaries normally are aware of their own altruism but not of the social and cultural disruption they sometimes cause. The people affected perceive the disruption immediately felt but can only deduce the motive. In the case of the United States, one might say that the Chinese communists exclude even the possibility of misguided benevolence and almost automatically look for a diabolical intention.

Both doctrine and emotions lead the Chinese to direct their anti-imperialist feeling primarily on the United States. Whatever the facts of earlier history were, the United States is and has been for two decades the centre of Western power. With regard to other Western nations, the passage of time and a relative decline in power have softened China's resentments. The European countries appear to the Chinese to have fallen into a status of subordination to the United States. To a certain extent this provides a basis for sympathy, if not for identification. The Chinese apparently still cling to an outmoded concept of relations among the capitalist countries, which other communists have modified with experience. They tend to magnify the differences between the United States and other Western countries, partly in the hope of profiting from them, partly because of unrealistic expectations. When disappointed in their expectations, they show chagrin but do not lose hope.

Direct assistance from Soviet bloc countries and other advantages China has derived from Soviet actions have disproportionately reinforced the Chinese sense of basic solidarity with world communism. China's disapproval of Western countries has not stopped her in dealing with many of them on a basis of expediency, as trade figures and the continued freedom of Hong Kong demonstrate. Neither does her identity with the Soviet bloc entirely override China's sense of national autonomy. With the development of disputes about world communist policy, the problem of Chinese national autonomy has become acute, precisely because of the strength of China's psychological commitment to bloc solidarity. This explains that inner tension so evident in the way the Chinese deal with the dispute, whereas their conflicts with non-communist countries imply no threat to the integrity of her current system of values.

Sino-Soviet Relations

Some observers of the Sino-Soviet relation have employed the analogy of a married couple. It has been asked whether the dispute would lead to reconciliation, separation, or divorce. The analogy seems rather more misleading than that of a set of brothers, which the Chinese themselves use. Their attitude toward the dispute may be better understood on the model of sibling relations in the Chinese family than on the model of spouse relations. The fraternal bond allows room for strongly charged mutual hostilities, even for the split of a family into two competing houses. But it is a blood bond, less easily broken and less subject to final dissolution than a marriage bond. Some tacit premises of Chinese culture, not shared or not considered relevant by the Russians, may thus have affected the political relationship between the two.

Chinese statements that the relations between communist countries are of a new and special kind are not to be taken as mere propaganda. Similarly, bodily analogies—the Sino-Vietnamese relation is said to be as close as that between the lips and the teeth—should not be too readily discounted. Such hyperbolical expressions are at their most frequent in periods of intra-bloc tension. They are rarely found in comments on third countries with which China maintains or hopes to establish co-operative relations. The Chinese orientation toward such third countries has been less categorical and

has varied more than their orientations toward the West and
the Soviet bloc.

China's views of the West reflect both the biographies of
the Chinese communist leaders and the facts of the distribution
of power. They have varied little over time. Her leaders have
dealt with the West, especially the United States, on the
premise that a permanent mutual antagonism exists, which
might be moderated by rather far-reaching changes in Western
behaviour, but which is likely to be resolved finally only
through conflict. They have recognized that the West is not a
single uniform entity, and though they have modified their
outlook on Western countries in accordance with their own
reading of recent history, they still believe only drastic methods
can remove the barrier between China and the West. China's
basic orientation to the Soviet Union and the Soviet bloc has
likewise been consistent. Central to it is the concept of a special
kind of solidarity, fraternal in nature. Conflicts within the
fraternity endanger the common good—something that can
never be at stake in conflicts with the West.

Third Countries in the Two-world Struggle

China's orientation to third countries, belonging neither to
the Eastern nor the Western camp, has been more variable.
In the early years of the Chinese People's Republic, the position
of such countries was viewed as anomalous. The Chinese took
the position that such countries must make a choice, even
regarding refusal to make the choice as an act inimical to
China and the Soviet bloc. At a later period, the Chinese
emphasized the common interests between themselves and such
third countries and affirmed the existence of mutual sympathy
based on common experience and a resulting common outlook.
In some of the authoritative Chinese statements, like the
communiqué of the Tenth Plenum of the Eighth CCP Congress,[2] the Chinese spoke of a joint movement with third
countries against 'neo-colonialism' and imperialism. This may

be a trend in international affairs of equal importance with East-West conflict, and possibly of greater importance.

Such variations can be explained in realistic terms. The earlier positions were designed to use the third countries to communist benefit in the 'two-world' struggle. The recent variation proposes to use them to China's benefit in the intra-bloc conflict as well as the total international arena. The antagonisms that have developed between China and India or Yugoslavia are partially explicable as part of a Chinese campaign to win the esteem and support of neutralism, which India and Yugoslavia also covet. But the whole set of variations seems to depend on preconceptions derived from China's own experience.

First, the Chinese communists have argued persistently that their revolution was the classical model for revolutions in underdeveloped countries. This implies that the Chinese conceive of social-political evolution in such countries as unilinear, a concept which is inconsistent with their own emphasis on the adaptation of Marxism to national circumstances. Another implication is that the Chinese will evaluate the political state of third countries by comparison with the stages through which their own revolution proceeded rather than in terms of the actual social-political structure of third countries.

Second, the Chinese tend to see the key social-political group in the third countries as the 'national bourgeoisie' (a term that applies rather closely to the group some Western scholars call the 'new middle class') and to see this group as ultimately entering into conflict with the 'proletariat'. Though the Chinese have never said so, they seem to think an Ah Q exists in every underdeveloped country and must be fought. They surely think that in every underdeveloped country there lurks a Chiang Kai-shek. They have made the direct comparison between major Asian-African leaders and Chiang at least twice in recent years. After the Iraqi revolution of 1958, when Nasser drew away from the Soviet Union and criticized Arab communists, the Chinese in an authoritative commentary[3] compared his actions with those of Chiang in 1927. Their conclusion, evidently addressed primarily to Arab audiences, was that the analogy proved that 'an anti-Soviet and anti-communist stand is fundamentally irreconcilable with the interests of national liberation'. More recently, coincidentally with the Chinese military advance into India's Northeast Frontier Agency, in another authoritative article[4] a similar comparison was made between Nehru and Chiang. This time the intended audience was possibly the Soviet Union as well as India and the neutral countries. The Chinese thus seem to believe that in all third countries, as in China, a domestic as well as an anti-colonial struggle must take place, and in the struggle the primacy of political methods and objectives must be honoured.

Third, the Chinese profoundly mistrust and misunderstand nationalism in the underdeveloped countries. A nationalist movement directed at achieving full and free expression in terms of indigenous cultural values is to the Chinese a 'bourgeois nationalist' movement. The attempt to preserve indigenous cultural values in the face of the social changes brought about by Western contact is, in truth, a difficult undertaking, but is, to say the least, legitimate. To the Chinese it is a diversion from the main political object of 'carrying the revolution through to the end', that is, of transferring power to the class which they approve. They regard bourgeois nationalist movements as having a 'progressive function for a certain period', but their relationship to such movements is clearly a temporary alliance.

Use of Information

To document these points, other than by quotation from ideological statements, is not easy. In analyzing the foreign outlook of most countries, one obvious thing to do is to review what the public media of communication have to say. In the

Chinese system, as in other totalitarian systems, information is used as an instrument of organization. Information about foreign countries as given to the public is highly selective. An interesting exercise, which anyone can do himself, is to summarize the output of the New China News Agency (NCNA) concerning a particular country over a set period. The political bias of the information selected is usually obvious.

In countries where there are organized groups favourably disposed toward China or toward the Chinese position on international issues, a major part of Chinese reportage is usually devoted to the activities of these groups. For countries like Burma and Cambodia, such reportage may constitute nearly all the content of NCNA coverage of the country for weeks at a stretch. On the other extreme, NCNA coverage of Thailand in recent years has emphasized alleged U.S. military and economic domination and so-called cultural imperialism almost to the exclusion of all other material. Reportage on Japan combines both extremes: over-reporting of the activities of organized groups favouring a more pro-Chinese policy of Japan alternates with all-out criticism of the Japanese government, especially of any of that government's activities in co-operation with the United States. Granted that Japanese political attitudes display a high degree of polarization, Japan is not so sharply divided a country nor are centrist positions so utterly absent as Chinese news treatment might lead a reader to suppose.

The political functions of such selective reporting are fairly clear. There is some value, though perhaps no urgent necessity, for the régime in keeping before the eyes of the Chinese public images of foreign countries consistent with the attitude the régime finds it useful to adopt toward them. The attention the Chinese give to pro-Chinese activities by foreign groups is doubtless a kind of psychological reward which helps to keep such groups active. Where the Chinese do not have direct communication with other countries or their governments, their statements serve as a cue indicating the sort of relations with those countries that China would accept or reject. Selectivity in news presentation, however, does not directly prove much about China's foreign outlook. It does to some extent confirm a proposition stated above—that the Chinese interest in other countries is narrowly, if not exclusively, political.

Ideological Formulations—Basic Convictions

News output, further, clearly does not contain all the information the régime possesses about other countries or the processes by which the Chinese interpret this information. On occasion, especially at times of tension, Chinese statements reveal information not contained in ordinary news output or supply a comprehensive interpretation of information previously published. The article about Nehru, cited above, is a case in point. Some earlier examples are to be found in Chinese discussions of Japanese affairs in November 1959, at a time when signing of the U.S.-Japanese Security Treaty was anticipated. This technique of controlled release of information, even more evident in some of the large-scale propaganda campaigns the Chinese have conducted from time to time, naturally leads one to suspect a profound cynicism on their part. One might guess that they have a much more sophisticated appreciation of reality than they reveal, and that they have a masterly ability to conceal their knowledge for deceptive purposes. But many students think, to the contrary, that especially at times of tension the Chinese reveal their actual calculations and that the heavily ideological formulations they issue at such times represent basic convictions. Many serious Japanese observers, for example, believe that despite all the facilities the Chinese have for gathering and analysing information on Japanese affairs, their views of Japan are based largely on the interpretations furnished them by Japanese Marxists.

A more accurate reflection of Chinese methods of appraisal might be expected to appear in the reports of foreign visits by important Chinese personalities, especially when these are made to a selected, high-level audience. On examination, these turn out to be as limited, as stereotyped, and as much adapted to the régime's current foreign political tactics as are mass communications. As an example, Chou En-lai, in reporting in March 1957 to the National Committee of the Chinese People's Political Consultative Conference,[5] described seven nationalist countries in Asia in terms that were almost identical from one case to another. In each case, he found that the country contained natural beauty and glorious ancient monuments; that its people admired China; that (with the partial exception of Pakistan) they cherished independence and peace on terms approved by the Chinese; and that since independence they had been able to advance in national construction. Similarly, Liu Chang-sheng in July 1961, in reporting on a four-month visit to eight African countries,[6] had little more to say than that they welcomed the Chinese warmly, were determined in their opposition to colonialism, and were developing their national economies since independence. In October 1961, Kuo Mo-jo reported to the Standing Committee of the National People's Congress on a visit to Indonesia and Burma by a delegation of the NPC.[7] Although his report was more circumstantial than the others cited in detailing natural beauties and cultural monuments, the content was again much the same as the earlier reports. He dwelt, as usual, on the warm and friendly feelings of his hosts toward the Chinese, their post-independence achievements in construction, and their anti-imperialist zeal. As a matter of significant detail, Kuo's reference to the monumental temple of Borobudur is worth quoting. He described it as a brilliant work of art by the Indonesian people, demonstrating the fathomless wisdom of the masses. He predicted that in the future they would be able to build more and better construction projects. The contention that great cultural monuments are a product of mass rather than individual effort is worth noting.

Tactical Requirements

These hackneyed travelogues are no more revealing than the mass communications media. They appear equally adapted to the tactical needs of the régime's foreign policy; and they reflect in the same way an outlook on foreign countries that produces observations only of what is politically relevant in the narrow sense. It is incredible that the Chinese leaders should be so insensitive to the cultural and historical backgrounds and to the actual shape of the national aspirations of countries with which they seek co-operative relations. This is especially surprising in men like Chou En-lai and Kuo Mo-jo. Chou's skill as a negotiator is well known. Kuo has shown an unusual facility in using words and gestures to produce the exact effect he wants with foreign audiences. This apparent lack of sensitivity is inconsistent with their ability to make foreign visitors feel at home. Japanese visitors regularly comment on the ease with which the Chinese, especially as contrasted with the Russians, establish rapport with them.

One explanation of these apparent anomalies is that public communications even to select audiences in China are, in effect, censored, and that fuller, more objective information is circulated to restricted government or CCP circles. This could be proved only when and if such documents come to light. Or one may assume that there is a carryover from earlier times of a tendency to view non-Chinese as barbarians, whose aspirations are of no intrinsic interest. The Chinese have sharply condemned 'great nation chauvinism'. Though they are conscious of the evil, they may be unable to control it. Dealing easily with people in direct face-to-face relations requires an ability to manipulate the superficial aspects of situations, but this is not necessarily the same thing as achieving sympathetic understanding. In short, the Chinese may be clever, even astute, in handling people without having real insight. Finally one might argue that the primacy of politics in the Chinese revolutionary model corresponds to something real and important in the Chinese communist make-up. One would then conclude that the narrowly political Chinese communist perspective is genuine; that they have no real interest in others except the political. One would anticipate that when documents hitherto unpublished come to light, they will reflect the same preoccupation with politics in the narrow sense as shown in those already published.

The Problem of Tradition

In connection with this argument, a glance at the Chinese communist evaluation of Chinese culture is worth taking. There has been in Chinese communism a strong emphasis on modernization and industrialization, on catching up with the West. Mao Tse-tung has frequently described China as 'poor and blank', thereby designating the overcoming of poverty as a major goal of the national effort. From the data cited above, it appears that the Chinese regard material progress as a major goal of post-independence cultural achievement for third countries as well as for China herself, and believe that progress is contingent on political conditions.

In recent years, there has been an upsurge of discussion in China concerning the utilization of so-called 'cultural legacy', that is to say, of China's own past. The problem is a universal one and, as noted earlier, virtually an inescapable one for non-Western societies subjected to the impact of the West. Chinese discussion of this problem has taken some strange forms. An evidently extensive restudy of Chinese history has been conducted, and there seems to be a growing, officially encouraged, tendency to emphasize the continuity of post-revolutionary China with historic China. Such an emphasis, one suspects would not need to be encouraged if it had not at one time been denied expression. The earlier tendency had been to regard tradition as a form of bondage and the revolutionary function as one of breaking this bondage by destroying and replacing the political system which was supposed to support and be supported by tradition. Mao's 'poor and blank' formula implies that revolution creates a *tabula rasa* and that this may be a good and productive condition. The more recent discussion has stressed, again with the support of appropriate quotations from

Mao's works, the desirability of preserving elements of tradition. One point is made emphatically, that those things should be preserved that directly promote the realization of the values established by the present régime. But it is hard to find in the various articles on the subject any understandable criteria of selection. The concept of evolution, either by natural adaptation or by directed reforms, from a traditional base has never been acceptable to Chinese communism. The use of tradition, then, is more a dilemma than a problem.[8]

Insight into alien cultures is never easy. For most people at all times, the normal attitude toward them is a naïve ethnocentrism. From this standpoint, alien cultures can be amusing or annoying but not much more. Among educated Westerners, the standpoint of cultural relativism has gained sufficient currency to make ethnocentrism at least unfashionable. Ideally, the relativist standpoint emerges from an examination of one's native tradition as one variety of the historically known traditions. One then comes to see it as historically conditioned, subject to rational criticism and adaptation but not to total rejection. This seems to be a necessary condition for genuine cultural tolerance.

Wholesale acceptance of a foreign tradition normally occurs only in personalities alienated from and hostile to their own. The conversion of the Chinese communists belonged to this class of phenomena. Political success validated their conversion. It also produced a new form of ethnocentrism, not entirely naïve but rationalized in terms of doctrine. The new ethnocentrism still persists and still strongly influences China's foreign outlook. That the Chinese can now encourage studies of the problem of cultural legacy may be a sign of maturity in internal politics. A similar growth in respect to external affairs seems as yet to be wanting.

Narrow Perception

It is perhaps in these terms that we can best understand the characteristic features of the Chinese communist foreign outlook—their dualism, their moral absolutism, the intensity of their anti-Westernism and the particular quality of their sense of solidarity with the socialist camp, their advocacy of their own revolutionary model as a guide to the underdeveloped countries, and their narrow perceptions of existing conditions in other countries. This is not to say that these observations make possible a complete account of Chinese foreign policy. What one can expect from analysis on the level adopted in this chapter is not that it will account for the tactical choices of action in situations where considerations of reality are clear-cut and determinative. Where self-preservation is at stake, as in the recent food shortage, the Chinese, like anybody else, will deal with the most satisfactory available supplier. For reasons of common sense, supported by doctrinal reasons, they do not undertake actions whose failure can be reasonably foreseen.

What can be expected of the observations made here is that the Chinese will delimit the range of behaviour in foreign relations characteristic of present-day Communist China. Since many of the situations that arise in international relations are ambiguous, there will be occasions when an underlying attitude will affect decision-making, perhaps critically. While China will not indefinitely tolerate the sacrifice of concrete national interests for the sake of bloc solidarity, Chinese calculations as to when these two interests conflict with each other are based on a scale of values different from that of Western nations. Perhaps one of the clearest measures of the influence of underlying attitudes is the Chinese method of calculation of the relative values of immediate and distant-future advantages. The Chinese are less inclined to accept immediate advantages at the potential cost of future disadvantages and more inclined to make present sacrifices in the hope of future gains than are most countries. Furthermore, the Chinese apparently see this kind of calculus as applicable in situations where others do not.

Finally, one must ask how deep-seated these Chinese attitudes are, when and how they may change, and how they affect the prospects of other countries in maintaining relations with China. We have spoken earlier of the biographical roots of Chinese attitudes. In the course of time, the present leaders will be succeeded by men with different life-patterns. Until that change takes place, or until domestic conditions force a sharing of power with Chinese of different tempers, only a drastic change in the environment will bring about a re-evaluation by the present leaders of their basic premises. The Sino-Soviet dispute might bring this to a head. As we have seen, there have been some hints that the Chinese are capable of contemplating a substitution of the underdeveloped world for the Soviet bloc as primary partners. Whether they could actually carry through such a course may be doubted. Even without changing basic premises, China has modified her relations with others and can do so again. There are always some minimal interests common to countries, no matter how incompatible. Critical analysis of China's basic attitudes can help to distinguish what are the real and the only apparent interests other countries have in common with China.

NOTES

[1] New China News Agency (NCNA), Peking Radio, 11 October 1958.

[2] See *Peking Review*, 39, 28 September 1962.

[3] Yu Chao-li, 'Imperialism is the sworn enemy of Arab national liberation', in *Hung-ch'i* (Red Flag), 7, 1 April 1959; translation in *Peking Review*, 14, 7 April 1959.

[4] 'More on Nehru's Philosophy in the light of the Sino-Indian boundary controversy', *Jen-min Jih-pao* (People's Daily), 27 October 1962; translation in *Peking Review*, 44, 2 November 1952.

[5] Chou En-lai, 'A report on visits to eleven countries in Asia and Europe', Supplement to *People's China*, 7, 1 April 1957.

[6] Peking Radio, 1–5 August 1961.

[7] Peking Radio, 10 October 1961.

[8] While it is unfair to select any single article as representative, the tortuous reasoning of Wu Chiang's 'On the question of study and criticism of cultural legacy', in *Hung-ch'i* (Red Flag), 6, 16 March 1961, translation in *Excerpts from China Mainland Magazines*, 255, may illustrate the nature of the dilemma.

CHAPTER TEN

TREATMENT OF MINORITIES

GEORGE N. PATTERSON

Members of the United Nations which have or assume responsibilities for the administration of territories whose people have not yet attained a full measure of self-government recognise the principle that the interests of the inhabitants of these territories are paramount, and accept as a sacred trust the obligation to promote to the utmost . . . the well-being of the inhabitants of these territories, to this end . . . to ensure just treatment, and their protection against abuses . . .'

United Nations Charter, Article 73–B.

In many instances, this obligation embodied in the U.N. Charter has been disregarded and not least in Asia where many minorities were denied their rights to self-government. After World War II, when nationalism was the driving political force in emancipating the new states, the nationalists often claimed sovereignty over the same territorial areas as the governments they had replaced. In taking over they usually refused to allow their lesser nationalist groups a right to self-determination and sought instead to absorb them, either establishing an absolute rule over the minorities or granting them less autonomy than what the latter demanded. Several of the new Asian states viewed any demand for autonomous rule a crime against the nation.

China emerged as the most formidable among these Asian monolithic states, expanding progressively her frontiers. She used greatly varied techniques in handling the national minorities, which China had enveloped in process of her historic expansions. Dr Sun Yat-sen had said that, under China's traditional absolutism, the people once they had discharged their obligations towards the state, were very much left like 'loose sand', to themselves; and Mao Tse-tung stated in the Constitution of the Kiangsi Soviet Republic of 1931:[1]

The Soviet Government of China recognizes the right of self-determination of the national minorities in China, their right to complete separation from China and to the formation of an independent state for each national minority. All Mongolians, Tibetans, Miao, Yao, Koreans and others living on the territory of China shall enjoy full right of self-determination, i.e. they may either join the Union of Chinese Soviets or secede from it and form their own state as they may prefer.

Since 1931, the Party has made many ambiguous declarations and several shifts in its policies concerning the national minorities. The promised right of secession was short-lived once the Party was in power. The *People's Daily* of 2 October 1951, in an editorial stated:

At this juncture, any national movement which seeks separation from the Chinese People's Republic for independence will be reactionary since, objectively considered, it would undermine the interests of the various races and particularly the foremost majority of the race concerned, and thus would work to the advantage of imperialism.

This statement became official Party policy with the adoption of the General Programme for the Implementation of Nationality Regional Autonomy on 8 August 1952. Article II states:

Each national autonomous area is an inseparable part of the territory of the People's Republic of China. . . . The autonomous organ in each autonomous area is a level of local government under the unified leadership of the Central People's Government and is led by the higher Government level.

In mid-1962, a conference in Peking sat for a month to discuss the achievements and experiences gained during the past years among China's national minorities. It was convened by the Nationalities Committee of the National People's Congress and the Nationalities Affairs Commission of the State Council; it was attended by representatives of 31 nationalities from 22 municipalities, provinces and autonomous regions; many leading members of the Communist Party and Government were present.

There was a great deal of self-congratulation, since the socialist construction of the minority areas was attributed to the Three Red Banners, i.e. the General Line for the building of 'socialism', the Great Leap Forward, and the People's Communes. How to handle correctly relationships between the various nationalities, always in conformity with the policies laid down by the Communist Party and Chairman Mao, was greatly stressed. The Party's policies were to encourage: enthusiasm and initiative in the development of agriculture, animal husbandry, forestry and improvement of living standards; instituting national regional autonomy; training of cadres from among the minority peoples; strengthening of the united front; freedom of religious belief; 'the special characteristics of the various nationalities'; and trade, education and public health.[2]

In practical terms, is this only a successful 'paper policy' designed to mask the alienation and suppression of the minorities' rights?

Integrating Ethnic Minorities

In 1949 when the Chinese communists came to power, they announced a policy of regional autonomy for the ethnic minorities. This seemed to be a great break with China's past record, for throughout her modern history, the central governments strove to integrate her minorities within the dominant Han majority. The new self-determination policy promised administrative, economic, educational and cultural rights. Article 53 in the *Common Programme* of the Chinese People's Political Consultative Conference guaranteed the development of minority languages and dialects. In 1950, the research facilities and personnel in this field were so limited that only a few minority languages could be considered and only thirty-two students enrolled. In 1954 however, capable personnel had been massively increased and a new policy was adopted. First, in areas where the population had its own dialects but did not possess a written language, assistance was to be given to formulate a phonetic language; secondly, regardless of whether or not a minority group had its written language it was 'free' to adopt the Chinese or any other language actually used in China.

In 1956, an editorial in the *People's Daily* of 3 February said that the unequal stages of development of the national minorities' languages 'retard education and production' and urgently recommended that this should be remedied; that out of some 40 million people 20 millions were affected by this linguistic retardation. Five years later, in 1961, the efforts to carry out these early promises and policies had nearly all been given up except in name. Scientific investigation into the spoken languages of the minorities seems also to have been stopped. The programme was finally buried in the Great Leap Forward, which marked the beginning of an all-out Hanization and communization of the national minorities.[3] The following surveys of the border regions of Mainland China show how much the minority rights have been suppressed.

TIBET

On 5 August 1950 General Liu Po-ch'eng (subsequently Marshal), chairman of the South-west China Military Commission, was thus quoted in a release of the New China News Agency: 'The People's Army will soon liberate Tibet. . . . When the country has been liberated Tibetans will be given regional autonomy and religious freedom. . . . The Communists will respect existing customs . . . lamas will be protected . . .'.[4] This was already a big step back from the 1931 declaration of 'the rights of self-determination . . . and complete separation from China . . . and an independent state for each national minority . . .'. But still it might be interpreted as a fairly reasonable and even legitimate policy, as it was by India, for instance, at the time. This policy was confirmed in the 17-Point Agreement of May 1951 signed between a Tibetan delegation and the Peking Government.

But the Dalai Lama, Tibet's spiritual and temporal ruler, in a statement on 20 June 1960, said that Peking had ignored the terms of the agreement, which he moreover claimed had been forced on what had been only a Goodwill Tibetan Mission to Peking, and it was stamped with a faked Tibetan seal; and that the Chinese Advisory Delegation became almost immediately Peking's instrument of political control.

China now bent every effort in building a trunk road into Tibet for the main and almost sole use—even in Chinese publicity—of military vehicles carrying troops and supplies. Such a large influx of Chinese mouths into this region with its precariously balanced food situation probably led to the Chinese decision to begin drastic reforms of the archaic Tibetan methods of food storage, supply and distribution. Since these methods were connected with the granary rights of monasteries, and with landownership and hereditary tax levies, the Chinese authorities began a campaign against monasteries and land-owners. This process, which started in 1952 in Kham,[5] was intensified in 1958 following the outbreak of the revolt in East Tibet,* and was 'completed' in the post-revolt period in 1960–62.† The Dalai Lama, who had fled to asylum in India during the revolt, held a press conference in Mussorie, India, on 20 June 1959. He was asked: 'Is it true that a deliberate and precise campaign has been conducted by the Chinese in Tibet against the Tibetan religion?' He replied:[6]

The report is correct in stating that, until 1958, over one thousand monasteries were destroyed, countless lamas and monks killed and imprisoned, and the extermination of religion actively attempted. From 1955 onwards a full-scale campaign was attempted in the provinces of Ü and Tsang for the full-scale extermination of religion. We have documentary proof of these actions and also of actions against the Buddha himself, who had been named as a reactionary element.

On 11 April 1956 the Chinese authorities in Peking announced:[7]

---

* 'All the monasteries are reactionaries under religious guise. They are instruments of exploitations, the stronghold of autocratic feudal lords who stand in the way of progressive socialistic production and they are the centre of rebellion against reform. . . . If they are completely destroyed then the autocratic feudal oppression and exploitation can be destroyed . . .'— quotation from the Tibetan-language newspaper, *Karzey Nyinrey Sargyur*, published by Chinese authorities and cited as an example of the Chinese attack on religion by International Commission of Jurists, in the *Question of Tibet and the Rule of Law*, Geneva 1959: 41.

† 'A democratic reform movement was launched in Tibet after the armed rebellion . . . a campaign was launched in the mountains . . . and a system of democratic administration was introduced. This movement has now been completed in the main . . .' *Jen-min Jih-pao (People's Daily)* 25 May 1962.

Peking's Banks have been opened in Lhasa, Shigatse, Chamdo and other places and in the previous four years have issued more than one million seven hundred thousand yüan of non-interest agricultural loans, and more than one hundred thousand yüan of non-interest pastoral loans, as well as various amounts of low-interest handicraft and commercial loans. One hundred thousand farm implements have been issued and two million yüan's worth of tea, cloth and daily necessities. Finally seven primary schools have been established with a total enrolment of two thousand Tibetan students. . . . Broadcasting stations have been set up in various cities and towns. Four thousand Chinese medical workers have been sent to Tibet, with five million yüan for hygienic enterprises. Hospitals have been built in Lhasa, Shigatse, Chamdo, etc. . . .

But at the same time Tibetan leaders protested:[8]

The Chinese communists are destroying all our customs and systems. . . . Since the occupation of Tibet by the Chinese communists all the former organizations of the Government have ceased to function and the Chinese communists have established a large number of illegal organizations in their place. . . . The Chinese communists have also established organizations such as the 'Patriotic Youth League' and 'Chinese Schools', with the sole object of indoctrinating the youth of Tibet in communism and thus to destroy the civilization and culture of the nation. . . .

In mid-1958 twenty thousand Khambas in East Tibet, short of food and ammunition after about two years of fighting, fell back on central Tibet and with the help of sympathizers there were given fresh supplies of food, arms and ammunition. These groups spread through south and south-west Tibet, with many more joining them, and the 'local' revolts became a national uprising. For a time, by threatening to bomb the Dalai Lama's palace, the Chinese authorities were able to keep Lhasa itself quiet and the news of the seriousness of the revolt from the Indian officials there. But with the dramatic flight of the Dalai Lama from Lhasa, the revolt, after a sudden, very temporary triumph, died from lack of ammunition and outside support.

However, the resistance continues. On 9 March 1964, the eve of the fifth anniversary of the Tibetan uprising against the Chinese, the Dalai Lama appealed to all 'freedom loving peoples of the world' not to forget the people of Tibet.

He said that thousands of Tibetans had been massacred, thousands rendered homeless and thousands more had escaped to neighbouring states, adding: 'But the barbarous atrocities, even to the extent of exterminating the race and the religious belief of Tibetans, still continue, and the struggle of the people still goes on'.

SINKIANG

Turkestan was made into a Chinese province, 'the new frontier area', in 1884 when Tso Tsung-t'ang in a brilliant campaign reconquered it from Yacob Beg, the leader of a Nationalist Islamic uprising. Sinkiang's communications are closer to the Soviet Union and Mongolia than with China proper, and its people, in majority Moslem Uighurs with Kazakhs, Uzbeks, Mongols and Russians, come from the same origins as the people over its northern and western borders. Sinkiang is thus geographically and racially inclined to the Soviet Union. But Peking has always made it clear that it is part of the Chinese People's Republic and in 1955 it became officially known as the Sinkiang Uighur Autonomous Region.

The Chinese Communist Party began its efforts to exercise control over the area in 1930 when the governor was a communist; but the latter did not approve of the Chinese Communist Party—he even put to death Mao Tse-tung's younger brother—and took his directives from the Communist International. On his retirement in 1944, a 'nationalist' revolt broke out, reputedly staged by the Soviet communists—but it remained local. Only in 1949, when the Chinese People's Army entered Sinkiang, did the Party begin to have some influence, however nominal at first. With time, as the Chinese influence spread throughout the province, the Soviet Union was gradually eased out.[9] To make up for this the Soviet Union strengthened its ties in the bordering Soviet Republics with increased aid to their agriculture and industries.

Between 1955–1960, Sinkiang made impressive progress thanks to Chinese technical supervision. A railway from Lanchow to Urumchi (Tehwa) was completed and several thousand miles of highways were built—one running into the Pamir highlands in the north. Among its vast resources, particularly in petroleum, non-ferrous metals, 'rare materials' and coal, the Chinese reported discovery of a Black Oil Mountain capable of supplying asphalt for all the provincial highways and western China. The report however did not specify the people who form-ed the labour force coming from the 'national minorities . . . who worked night and day on the highways and railways throughout the province'.[10] The Hong Kong reports said the labourers were recalcitrant provincials and people from distant frontier regions of China, sent to be 'reformed through labour' in this Chinese 'Siberia'.

The production figures given for Sinkiang are probably no less correct than for elsewhere in China. With its great potentials the province is of great strategic importance to China's economic and military policies and it is to Chinese interest to develop these resources to offset Soviet influence. Over ten thousand—(*i-wan* 一萬) is a common Chinese term for a great many—factories were built, according to reports, to produce heavy industrial products in preference to consumer goods—these in addition to local industries. Thermoelectric and hydroelectric stations, mines, iron and steel plants, petro-leum wells and refineries, and electro-motor factories were thus established. Agriculture reclaimed 5 million *mou* (there are 6·6 *mou* to an acre) of wasteland and 108 state-owned co-operatives and communes were set up.

Nevertheless in eastern parts of the province during 1958–1959 there was sporadic fighting, according to Tibetan guerilla leaders in the region. The Chinese communists have admitted that during those years there was great unrest throughout Sinkiang. As one report[11] said:

Important victories have been won in the anti-local nationalism struggle in various parts of the Sinkiang Uighur Autonomous Region. . . . Various Party committees fully used such methods as free airing of views, posting large-character wall-newspapers, and conducting free debates and forums; exposed and criticized the serious local nationalism existing within the Party; launched solemn struggles against parochial, nationalistic anti-Party cliques and individuals. . . . All those local nationalists exposed in various places had assaulted the Party in a ruthless manner in an attempt to oppose unification of the Fatherland, to sabotage the unity of nationalities . . . running against and debilitating proletarian dictatorship, counteracting and trying to seize Party leadership, and doing everything they could to substitute nationalism for socialism. . . .

The widespread revolt of the national minorities against Chinese oppression was blamed on the 'nationalists . . . who tried to find in history and in foreign countries the basis of establishing a "republic", hoping to tear Sinkiang away from the large family of the Socialist Fatherland'. In proof thereof the Party said the nationalists had demanded that the public security organs be staffed with more national minority people, that all the civil police should be minority nationals, and that Party members of minority origin be more numerous in the Party committees.

To counter this the Party decided to take strict measures to 'prevent the growth of bourgeois individualism'. If this were not overcome it could very easily develop into nationalism. This in turn would lead to the emergence of conservative antiforeignism and hostile feeling against other nationalities. On the question of minority regional autonomy and national unification, it would over-emphasize the rights of autonomy and ignore the unity of the country. It was necessary, therefore, to 'heighten Marxist-Leninist thinking and awareness and completely overcome local nationalistic ideas'.[12]

To ensure that the 'national minorities' co-operated with their 'Han instructors', General Chu Teh was sent to Sinkiang to review progress of the Sinkiang Uighur Autonomous Military Region. He ordered that the Production Army Corps should, in addition to their normal military duties, 'also do their best to participate in production and construction in the border region, particularly in the building of railways. At the same time the tactics of the Sinkiang Military Region should be to train troops, cultivate cadres, organize and drill militiamen'.[13]

Recent reports speak of further outbreaks of revolt on a wide scale in both Sinkiang and East Tibet.[14] On 9 June 1963 the

Hong Kong *Sunday Post Herald* reported an uprising in Sinkiang early in 1962 in which Kazakhs, Uighurs and Uzbeks marched on the Russian Consulate in Kuldja and demanded arms to 'drive out the Chinese' after twelve persons had been killed the previous day by Chinese troops. Many subsequently fled across the border into Russia.

The *People's Daily* of 6 September 1963 charged that Soviet personnel carried out 'large-scale' subversive activities in this region in 1962 and 'enticed and coerced several tens of thousands of Chinese citizens into going to the Soviet Union'. The article added, 'The Chinese Government lodged repeated protests and made repeated representations, but the Soviet Government refused to repatriate the Chinese on the pretext of "the sense of Soviet legality and humanitarianism". To this day, this incident remains unsettled'.

On 21 September in an official government statement the Soviet Union charged that Chinese military men and civilians had been 'systematically violating' the Soviet border since 1960. 'In the single year 1962, more than 5,000 violations of the Soviet border from the Chinese side were recorded', the statement added.

Other unverified reports of concentration camps in Sinkiang, large-scale Chinese troop revolts and massing of troops on both sides of the Sinkiang border followed. In February 1964, Soviet and Chinese officials met in Peking to seek common ground for discussing their border problems.

' . . . MIAOS AND OTHERS'

A conference on 'nationalities work' was convened by the Yünnan Nationalities Affairs Committee in July-August 1962. It discussed the experience and achievements over the past twelve years of Chinese communist policies concerning the regional autonomy of six million people among minority nationalities in Yünnan, and their future assignments according to the Central Government's directions. There were present delegates from 110 autonomous countries. The report was almost in identical terms with those from other minority areas:

Based on the policies on minority nationalities as laid down by the Chinese Communist People's Central Committee each locality through-out the province has made sincere efforts to strengthen the solidarity among various nationalities, promote regional autonomy in national minority areas, increase the number of national minority cadres, etc. . . .[15]

Very significant however was the emphasis put on future policy with regard to religious belief among minority nationalities; while this should be respected 'there must be constant vigilance against sabotage by counter-revolutionaries under the cloak of religion'. The Conference also said it was important 'to develop friendly relations between the Chinese People's Republic and the neighbouring nations of Burma, Laos, and North Vietnam'.[16]

The Himalayan Border States

At the beginning of 1962 a new Chinese policy in Tibet and the Himalayan Border States was formulated to offset the bad image created—in the case of Tibet—by previous policies, and—in the case of the neighbouring Himalayan territories—by the ruthless suppression of the Tibetan revolt.

The first official statement on this new policy in Tibet is found in a *Peking Review* article of 8 June 1962. After an introductory analysis of the many evils of 'the reactionary upper strata responsible for the revolt', it says: 'The war was one between the revolutionary classes and the counter-revolutionaries and certainly not one between nations'. Chang Ching-wu, secretary of the Chinese Communist Party in Tibet and representative of Peking in Lhasa, in his outline of the new policy on 'the united front', said: 'In the revolutionary struggle in Tibet united front work is of the utmost importance. . . . The united front, however, had serious limitations before democratic reform'. In practice this was interpreted to mean, in the sphere of religion, that the rigorous policy of eliminating the monastic system should be modified and the removal of lamas for 'constructive labour reforms' (in the above article referred to as 'reforms . . . firmly carried out according to the principle of political unification and religious principle') changed to a more co-operative policy. Regional autonomy was propagated again: 'National regional autonomy is an essential sign of the realization of equality and unity among nationalities. *It means that a national minority administers its own affairs*'. [Italics mine, quoting from the same article.]

At the same time Chang stated that the former Tibetan local government, which was dissolved as a consequence of the revolt, would not be reconstituted and the Preparatory Committee for the Autonomous Regions of Tibet would be entrusted with the new policy to be carried out, with the help of 'a certain number of cadres of Han and other nationalities'.

From 1956 onwards, after some hesitant starts, Peking made local offers of 'autonomy' for Darjeeling-Dooars District (the famous tea-growing area was infiltrated by communist agitators), in a 'federation of Sikkim and Bhutan and "Gurkhastan"', which would also include Nepal and the three million Nepalis living in North Bengal and Northern Assam. These offers in 1962 emerged as a policy to establish a 'Confederation of Himalayan States', to be formed by Nepal, Sikkim, Bhutan, the North East Frontier Area of India and Nagaland.[17]

Nepal is the least 'disturbed', politically speaking, among the Himalayan territories bordering China. This is partly due to the King's use of 'direct rule'; its U.N. membership and a diplomatic corps at Kathmandu of foreign powers among which are those of the Soviet Union and the Chinese People's Republic; and also of foreign aid, more indeed than the country can fully use at the moment. Aid from China came in the form of a strategic road from Lhasa to Kathmandu and economic grants totalling 140 million Indian rupees. In the light of China's great interest in Nepal, Mao Tse-tung's words are worth recalling: 'In defeating China in war the imperialists have taken away many dependent Chinese states and a part of her territories. . . England seized Burma, Bhutan, Nepal and Hong Kong . . .'.[18]

Sikkim is a small 2,800-square-mile kingdom with a population of 165,000, almost 100,000 of whom are Nepalis subject to political influences from Nepal; the remainder of the population is divided between Lepchas, Bhutias and Tibetans. The ruling family is of Tibetan extraction. Although only a small Himalayan state, it has been described in *Tibet Past and Present* (1924) by Sir Charles Bell as 'a dagger thrust at the heart of India' because of its strategic position between Tibet and India's industrial heartland.

Until Britain installed a Maharajah, who died late in 1963 and was succeeded by his son, China claimed suzerainty over Sikkim, under broadly the same provisions as Nepal and Bhutan. China still maintains that Sikkim and Bhutan are not India's responsibility, and they were pointedly excluded from the Sino-Indian Boundary Commissions discussion.

Bhutan is a mountain and jungle-slashed region of approximately 18,000 square miles with an estimated population of approximately 700,000. It lies in the strategic area between Sikkim and Burma, south of Tibet. The people are of Tibetan extraction, although in recent years several thousand Nepalis have made their way into the country. Traditionally, Bhutan has served as the 'granary of Tibet' and its racial and economic links with the north have created tensions inside Bhutan because of the present 'friendship with India' policy of the Maharajah and the Prime Minister. These tensions are being intensified by the Chinese who offer excellent prices for the food and goods banned by India, and who encourage the Bhutanese to take advantage of all educational, medical and technical facilities being offered to them across the border in Tibet. There are also reports that Bhutanese and Sikkimese who take advantage of these offers are being formed into 'émigré governments' and that China is putting pressure on Nepal and other neighbouring countries to recognize these régimes.[19]

India's North East Frontier Agency between Bhutan and Burma is claimed by China as part of her former dependencies and minorities.[20] She occupied some of it in 1960, and in 1962 entered the territory with 30,000 troops and laid a claim to all of it. The movement of tribes over the centuries has left the whole of this area with a predominantly Tibeto-Burmese people of Mongolian origin, with only a slight admixture of other races. From the area south of the North East Frontier Agency, the Nagas have conducted an eight-year revolt against India. Chinese interest in, and claims to, the North East Frontier Agency,[21] the Nagas,[22] and the Kachins of North Burma[23] indicate that whatever motives lie behind her proposals for a 'Confederation of Himalayan States', her eventual policy is to include them within her own jurisdiction.

The basic policy of China—despite its frequent declarations condemning 'great Han chauvinism' and its dangers—is still to return her former 'dependent territories' to their China 'motherland'. The Chinese Communist Party to make good this national commitment will use moderation and persuasion, but should these mean their purpose fails, it will ruthlessly apply coercion at all levels—military, administrative, economic and cultural.

Self-government and nation-self-expression have been denied to the national minorities despite all the Party's declarations, beginning with the Constitution of 1931 and reiterated in the *Common Programme* in 1949. This grand design of the Chinese Communist Party reaches well beyond the present borders of the China mainland as its military strength develops.

NOTES

[1] *China Quarterly*, **1** (January–March 1960): 92.

[2] *Peking Review*, **23** (8 June 1962): 3.

[3] *China Quarterly*, **12** (October–December 1962): 170–182.

[4] Patterson, George N., *Tragic Destiny*, p. 31.

[5] *Concerning the Question of Tibet*, Peking 1959.

[6] International Commission of Jurists, *The Question of Tibet and the Rule of Law* (Geneva 1959), Document 20: 200–1.

[7] *Shih-shih Shou-ts'e* (Current Affairs Handbook), Peking, 30 April 1956.

[8] *China Quarterly*, **1** (January–March 1960): 95.

[9] *Union Research Service* (Hong Kong), **13** (15): 207.

[10] *Ibid.*, 217.

[11] *Kuang-ming Jih-pao*, Peking, 11 September 1958.

[12] *Hsiang-chiang Jih-pao*, Urumchi, 6 September 1958.

[13] *Liberation Army News*, Peking, 26 September 1958.

[14] *Statesman*, Calcutta, 18 January 1963.

[15] *Yünnan Jih-pao*, report in B.B.C. *Summary of World Broadcasts*, 9 August 1962.

[16] *Ibid.*

[17] Patterson, George N., *Tibet in Revolt*, London 1960.

[18] *Ibid.*

[19] *China Quarterly*, **12** (October–December 1962).

[20] *Sino-Indian Boundary Question*, Peking, November 1962.

[21] *Ibid.*

[22] *China Quarterly*, **12** (October–December 1962).

[23] *B.B.C. Summary of World Broadcasts*, quoting Chinese Nationalist Report from Taipeh, 10 December 1962 and Rangoon Report, 15 November 1962.

CHAPTER ELEVEN

CREATING A RULING CLASS

JOHN BUSBY

A successful revolution has to have a group of leaders who become governors of the nation and turn into its ruling class, as their régime gets stabilized. Thus in 1921 a handful of Chinese intellectuals grouped themselves into a communist party and some of them have survived to rule Mainland China today and direct its destinies on the path described in other chapters of this book. This chapter is about how they trained themselves into rulers and organized a great mass of subordinates to carry out their plans, in other words how the Chinese Communist Party grew and got going.

To clear the ground, two introductory points should be made. First, for reasons of security and also to guard its prestige, the Party publishes little on its internal policies and problems except in general and often idealized terms. Whereas, for example, the economist has (or at least used to have) a mass of factual data with which to form a picture of Chinese economic policy, the political analyst describing how the Party really functions is forced to rely heavily on inference and to avoid too precise statements. Second, the Party is organized in order to transform China on communist lines; it is not part of the finished product, but a tool made specifically for the purpose of seizing power through class struggle and effecting rapid revolutionary changes in the whole fabric of society. It is, therefore, not part of the Chinese model which anyone without totalitarian ambitions would consider copying. This chapter is therefore not so much concerned to demonstrate the inadequacy of the Chinese model in this field as to show how completely it is adapted to totalitarian concepts of revolution. But even as a tool for the communist transformation of China the CCP has certain shortcomings; these will be mentioned.

How, then, has this new ruling class been formed in China? In forty years of leadership the leaders have never had a pause in the main tasks of expanding their power and of ruling China, which would allow them time to train a body of followers for the next campaign. Recruitment and organization was an integral part of each campaign, during which they educated themselves and trained their subordinates on the job from day to day and year to year. The formation of the CCP must therefore be studied through its successive historical periods, noting how the Party grew in numbers, what experience the leaders gained, and the particular lessons they impressed on their followers in different situations.

The Formative Years

Between 1921 and 1927 the Party grew from a handful of radical nationalists, young intellectuals who had just discovered Marxism-Leninism, into an organized Party of 59,000 with varied experience. Some of the future leaders, notably Liu Shao-ch'i, had launched the first militant labour movements in China and had led big strikes; others were graduating as communist intellectuals, recruiting students to the cause and fighting wordy battles in little magazines; others were working within the Nationalist Party—the Kuomintang—under the alliance concluded between Sun Yat-sen and the Soviet Union. The Nationalists had a territorial base in Canton and there Mao Tse-tung, Chou En-lai and their colleagues trained themselves in administration and propaganda, learnt how to train a modern army and how to recruit cautiously supporters within the larger organization which was suspicious of their activities. These various groups were bound together by the Party network which operated secretly in the areas controlled by the war-lords and the foreign powers. The Party therefore needed conspiracy and discipline to succeed.

In 1927 Chiang Kai-shek, alarmed by the growth of the Communist Party, attempted to wipe it out at one blow; and though he failed, he nevertheless did it grave damage, for Party members declined from 59,000 to 10,000. The rump of the Party was temporarily split; most of its leaders went underground in Shanghai and other big cities. Chou En-lai and others who survived a losing battle against the police learnt more of conspiracy, secrecy and the techniques of defence against internal traitors, but they also experienced the extent to which a radical opposition in China could count on help in the universities and from other intellectual groups. Half of the Party men collected into a number of rural bases in South China and learnt a different sort of politics. As a cadre in the Nationalist organization, Mao Tse-tung had been concerned in plans to stir up and organize the peasants to help the Nationalist forces advancing north. After the split Mao moved into a remote mountainous district, where he was joined by officers and men of the Nationalist forces who had rebelled after Chiang's coup. Within two years he led what was in effect a government of part of rural China: to achieve this he had to persuade peasants to receive the communist forces as friends with a right to levy taxes and enroll soldiers against the régime they were fighting. He appealed chiefly to the poor peasants, to whom the Party offered a bright though perilous future. An essential element in his policy was a harsh class line, which impoverished the landlords and also humiliated them to give the poor peasants self-confidence and prestige in the new régime.

Besides these problems of a revolutionary government in a desperate situation, Mao and his colleagues had also to solve military ones. Red troops, recruited largely from captured Nationalists, had to be kept fighting however few the weapons and poor the rations. The basic rules of guerilla warfare had to be learnt and in a situation of continuous war, trained officers had to learn to subordinate themselves to overall policies which often conflicted with their professional predilections. The whole enterprise was energized with revolutionary enthusiasm to elevate the poor against the rich oppressor and to make China

strong enough to thrust out the foreigner. Many of the most
pressing problems involved turning this basic enthusiasm into
a disciplined force which could hold together through thick and
thin and manoeuvre as a unit against hostile armies and political
alliances. To achieve this the leaders worked hard to gain
agreement on general policies and to instil the conviction that
strength demanded unity.

This first period of rural warfare developed the capacity of
the Party leaders to live amongst a conservative peasantry and
activate it. They also acquired simple administrative techniques,
notably in the collection and expenditure of money, and the
whole range of those capacities needed to wage war. War was
so much a part of Party activity in the little rural bases, and
military strategy so tied up with political strategy if the armies
were to survive, that the leaders appear to have shared political
and military authority to a degree which made it difficult to
distinguish the field officer from the political worker. The
Party expanded rapidly by taking in peasants both as soldiers
and as Party representatives in the villages where the class
struggle raged. From this time on the CCP has been divided
between a largely peasant base, men and women who owe
all their education and all opportunities for advancement to
the Party, and the intellectuals, who have acquired their mental
equipment independently of the Party. The first group is loyal,
but short-sighted and prone to relax when a little prosperity
is achieved. The second group are indispensable for strategy,
propaganda and diplomacy but prone to individualism and
bookishness.

Move to the Rural Areas

In about 1933 the Shanghai leaders were forced to move
out to the rural areas, where, by virtue of their seniority,
they could to a large extent replace Mao and his colleagues in
the direction of the rural bases. They committed serious
strategic errors and within two years had to relinquish the
overall leadership to Mao. Li Li-san, Moscow-trained, favouring
the urban *putsch* and military solution and over-violent in

dealing with dissident colleagues, is the eponym of the leadership displaced at that time; his case is still occasionally recounted when Mao deems that similar tendencies may need correction in the Party.

In 1935 under increased military pressure the Party had to move from the southwest to the new rural bases in northwest China which it was to occupy for over a decade. This geographical shift seems to have left the Party's situation and policies substantially unchanged; but two important developments occurred. First, the Japanese attack on China gave the Party a new enemy, and new fields from which to recruit its strength. Secondly, the temporary alliance with the Nationalists, forced upon them by the Japanese invader, enabled the Party to operate more or less openly in the cities, and so to challenge the Nationalists for the allegiance of the upper classes under Chiang's very eyes.

These new factors influenced the growth of the Party in experience and in numbers. The Japanese attack helped the Communist Party to make new recruits in two important fields. Continuing the process begun in the rural civil war, the Party expanded through the peasantry, creating ever bigger bases through north and central China and recruiting more and more peasant soldiers. Development was all the more rapid since foreign invasion made it easier for the Party to agitate and organize the poorer peasants than had been possible when the local landlords and Nationalist troops were the only enemies. Japanese aggression coupled with Nationalist failure to organize resistance behind the tenuous Japanese military lines created a situation where patriotism and working with communists became synonymous over much of China; and the communists worked hard to win over to communism those who started as their patriotic collaborators. Secondly, the patriotic call 'repel the invader' immensely increased the attractiveness of the Party to the already radical young intelligentsia. Students who had reason to be dissatisfied with the Nationalists' dilatoriness and inefficiency as a war party, flocked to Mao's banner in increasing numbers. This gave the Party a valuable source of talent, but brought new problems of how to use and then incorporate large numbers of middle class radicals with individualistic tendencies. During the war against Japan the Party grew rapidly, from 40,000 in 1937 to 1,210,000 in 1945.

Although the problem of the Party's organization and the training and control of widely scattered military forces and political bases remained the same during the war against Japan, the new scale of these problems made it necessary for Mao to put in writing the principles which should guide the Party, and to insist on unanimity in observing them. At the same time some relaxation in the day-to-day questions of survival gave the leaders leisure to work out their views in more detail and to organize extensive training courses. Stalin's own unprincipled attitude on Party organization may also have inclined Mao to give serious attention to these matters.

Following the Soviet Pattern

The principles which Mao laid down for the guidance of colleagues in their relations with each other and with the masses outside the Party were to a large extent taken from Soviet texts. The issues of centralism and democracy, discipline and initiative, subjectivism, dogmatism, and true Marxism-Leninism were all tackled on Soviet lines. However, in view of the differences between Stalin's practice and Soviet theory, Mao's writings on these problems cannot be relied on for hard information as to the actual life within the Party. Although Mao does not seem to have ignored his own precepts to the extent which Stalin did, there were considerable deviations from the idealized picture of inner-Party life which his directives suggest. The particular topics raised and the emphasis given to certain points do, nevertheless, indicate broadly how Chinese Party members were being trained at this time.

First, they were, like all communists, called on to accept a common view of the situation in China and the policies of the Party. This was presented to them as Mao's view. The CCP thus followed the pattern of the Soviet Party in accepting one man as titular leader. They were furthermore encouraged to see themselves as a Chinese Party, firmly rooted in Chinese history and free to make their own decisions as Chinese Marxists. Those who parroted Soviet texts in ignorance of the Chinese situation were one of the Party's main targets. The need to concentrate on practical Chinese facts re-emerged in the drive to convert the newly recruited intellectuals of bourgeois and urban backgrounds into useful Party workers capable of talking to and working on the peasant masses. At the same time the illiterate wing of the Party, the poor peasants in the villages and the armies, were given every encouragement to get an education and take the first steps towards the theory on which Mao and his colleagues claimed to base their policies. Finally, Mao and his colleagues dealt at length with the principles of intra-Party struggles, that is, the way in which disputes on policy should be conducted and the treatment of dissident minorities. They emphasized honest argument and the need to avoid overviolent and unprincipled attacks on defeated minorities. Although nothing was said to contravene Soviet precept, the fact that the Chinese should have done so shortly after Stalin's appalling purges suggests it was a deliberate attempt not to follow Russia in this matter. Party members were in effect given the assurance that so long as they filled the minimum requirements of honesty and loyalty they would not run the risk of the grievous wrongs then common in the Soviet Union. And this important guarantee has been generally honoured within the CCP.

When Japan surrendered in 1945, Communist China had a group of leaders and their educated lieutenants with practical experience in fighting, in the administration of rural areas and in winning over both peasants and urban intellectuals; a large army in which all the officers and many of the soldiers were Party members; and a growing force of peasant cadres who were gradually replacing, sometimes peacefully, sometimes

murderously, the landlord groups which had formerly dominated rural China. This formidable force returned to civil war
with little perceptible strain and change in strategy. There
was, however, one important political change. Whereas during
the war against Japan the Party had slowed down its land
reform and destruction of the landlord class, the process was
now accelerated. In village after village the Party worked
amongst the poorer peasants and put them in a mood to overthrow the ancient system. As the struggle developed, the Party
took into itself the peasants who had been most active in
following its leadership; the lower ranks of the Party were
mostly peasants.

The Party in Power

By 1950 the CCP had occupied the whole of mainland
China. After seizing power in war, Mao now had to use it in
peace and was faced with problems of recruiting, training and
organizing the Party cadres.

One big new problem came with peace itself. Whereas before
1949 the dangers and hardships of Party life ensured that those
who tried to join the Party were at least keen and courageous,
in the transition to peace the immediate problem was to keep
the Party free of ambitious opportunists and the ordinary
second-rate.

The great expansion in territory and the addition of huge
cities to what had been a rural empire meant also an increased
demand for young cadres. The Party solved this problem by
setting up temporary 'revolutionary universities' to give shock
courses to large numbers of students and younger members of
the old élite, notably civil servants and teachers. The courses
were partly intellectual in that they inculcated a knowledge
both of current Party policies and communist ideology, but
their more important purpose was psychological. Students
were isolated, worked to exhaustion, surrounded by vague
threats, and subjected to long hours of confession and mutual

criticism with the general idea of producing an intense revulsion against the old society and their own 'pre-communist' ideas, and to substitute instead a loyalty towards the Party and a zealous determination to further its policies. So far as one can judge, these courses were generally successful. They enabled the CCP to incorporate rapidly a considerable proportion of younger talent.

The transition from war to peace was not, however, so abrupt as to bring up in 1949 the problems of peace in their worst form. The Korean War provided a severe testing ground both for former Nationalist troops which had been reincorporated in mass into the Red Army and for enthusiastic students from the cities. Nearer home, the succession of revolutionary movements launched by the Party kept town and country in a state of unrest which, though not war, was a long way from peace as normally understood. In 1950 and 1951 land reform was spread through the 'newly-liberated' areas and continued to act as a training ground for both poor peasants and for left-wing students and military cadres, who were rapidly organized into teams to instigate and guide the liquidation of the landlords.

In the cities, the campaigns against labour bosses and against corruption amongst the merchants and the parallel drives against American influence in the universities and against the foreign missionary in every sphere of life provided tests for various urban strata (workmen, clerks, students, teachers and doctors). And the brutal pervasive drives to ferret out hidden and possible enemies provided sharp tests for loyalty and energy.

The Party continued to grow, from 2·7 millions in 1947 to 4·5 millions in 1949 and to 6 millions in 1953.

By about 1955 this succession of violent movements against imperialism, feudalism and 'capitalism' had run their course, and the Party began to consider the long and complex tasks of the development of China as a 'socialist' country.

Most of these tasks can be summed up in the slogan 'increase production', which became the prime concern of the majority of cadres in both town and country. Now production, that is to say day-to-day economic work, whether by the planner at his desk or the artisan at his lathe, requires a sort of discipline and outlook unlike that demanded by the tasks of war and propaganda with which the Party had been largely occupied. The leaders realized this in principle, and exhorted their subordinates to learn the secrets of a new and difficult world, but in practice the transition presented problems which still defy them.

In industry, commerce, education and other urban sectors 'increase production' involved many activities which would be recognized as normal in a non-communist country. Senior communists drafted into a factory, for example, immediately assumed part responsibility for its operation and had to learn enough of its techniques and managerial problems to get the most out of the workers, technical foremen and the managers themselves, and also to represent their factory in negotiations with the ministry and other superior organs. And, since the Party still wanted to get the cream of the nation into its own ranks, senior communists had the important task of recruiting for the Party outstanding men of all grades who seemed to fulfil the minimum requirements of zeal and loyalty. They also retained the general responsibility for the political health of their unit, the duty to make sure that their masses understood the current political scene and took part in the current movements. In education, the overall political tasks were relatively more important, since the rising generations were expected to emerge from school and university loyal and understanding servants of the Party as well as useful technicians. This requirement created constant tension in the schools between the requirements of technical instruction and of loyalty and zeal, between old teachers and new Party leaders. This question of the relationship between Party and old intellectuals will be dealt with later.

In agriculture the situation was even more complex since land reform was no sooner completed than the régime decreed a rapid advance to the collectivization of agriculture. The village had to be kept going as a farming unit able to feed itself and also meet stiff tax demands, while individually the peasant was being deprived of land and pushed into a farming system totally alien to China and of unproven value. This double task required a rare mixture of tact and vigour. The task force came apparently from the lower echelons of the Party of peasant origin, the young man who had joined to fight the Japanese and his brother who had learnt to fight his own landlord. Some faced their new assignment with success, that is to say they more or less persuaded the peasants to accept the new arrangements as a possible way forward, and to work with as much zeal for the collective as they had done on their own. The majority of cadres, however, simply ordered the peasants into collectives, and then found themselves the focus of the worst tensions in China, between a disturbed and apathetic peasantry and Party leaders who could scarcely tolerate any fall in tax receipts. As farm yields refused to show any substantial improvements the leaders first tried moderate measures. For the village cadres this meant a mild purge; the over-authoritarian cadres were removed but the great majority were kept. A sustained effort was made to get the system to work somehow by constant persuasion relieved with small concessions to the richer peasants who had lost most by collectivization but could contribute a good deal as farmers.

The Great Leap

This period of half measures ended with the Great Leap of 1958 and the early commune period. Instead of mild compulsion disguised as persuasion and mitigated by concessions to the wealthier peasants, the cadres found themselves directing a movement which, in violence of propaganda and scorn for concessions, must have carried them back to the stirring days of war and land reform. The aim was to sweep the whole country first into a feverish drive for production, and then into a large and egalitarian version of the collective farm, namely the commune. The method was utopian propaganda which virtually ignored both facts and possibilities; and all who held back whether from prudence, selfishness, or sheer conservatism were labelled rightist and shouted down.

The composition of the rural cadre force changed at this time as numbers of young urban cadres (students who had just left school and older intellectuals), were sent to the villages both to stiffen the original peasant force during the period of rapid change and to acquire something of the tempering which had helped greatly in the development of the Party during its strenuous youth of war and violent revolution. Rural China during the Leap constituted an admirable school for the urban élite, which knew little of rural China and less of revolutionary violence, but the practical results were not so glorious. War-time modes of operation failed when applied in disregard of the farmer's calendar. The cadres found that they could indeed drive or lead the peasants forward to perform prodigious tasks, but they tended to overdrive them, and to undertake extravagant projects for which rural China was still too poor; farm work requiring patience and devotion was neglected in preference to operations like digging canals where massive labour can make an immediate impact. The Party leaders began calling off this mad advance fairly quickly, but were faced with an appalling problem in helping the junior cadres to climb down in front of the misled peasants and yet maintain guidance and control at a lower pitch. This difficult retreat seemingly has been accomplished: the rural cadres are still in control, but back where they were before the Leap in a difficult world of patience, concession and persuasion, and disillusioned to find that there is no quick solution to China's rural problem.

Lifting our eyes from the base of the pyramid to its apex, we see that the policy changes involved in introducing and then abandoning the 1958 Leap caused a strain in the Party leadership greater than had ever been since Mao established his strategic policy and his personal position, about twenty years earlier. Several leaders at the centre, among whom Ch'en

Yün, the senior vice-premier, Teng Tze-hui, the vice-premier in charge of agriculture, P'eng Te-huai, the minister of Defence, and two successive chiefs of staff, the head of the Statistical Bureau and the head of the office controlling light industry, appear to have opposed the 1958 policies as rash and were pushed aside. At the provincial level the Party casualties were even more severe; about one-third of its secretaries were dismissed with contumely in 1957 and 1958, apparently for opposing the Leap, and a further group has recently suffered for the opposite fault of 'leaping' with such energy as to come down on the peasants with unbearable weight. This serious split and the consequent loss of talent leads one to the conclusion that the team which Mao led to victory in civil war, and the methods by which he forged unity at the top of the Party, failed to meet the different challenge of peace-time development and administration. Will he be able to hold out with what remains of his old team or must further drastic changes take place before a peace-time leadership is finally established? The reply lies in the future.

The Intellectuals

So far our assumption has been that in China the Party alone constitutes the 'ruling class'. But once the Party set itself to develop China it had to rely on the higher intellectuals, men of university education, in formulating and executing its programmes. Economic planning, the establishment of new industries and the development of science cannot be controlled by the Party in the way Mao and his colleagues controlled armies, the administration and the elementary economic structure of the civil-war period. These intellectuals, though without political power, nevertheless are part of the ruling class to the extent that the Party cannot rule without their skills. Our study therefore includes this lesser segment of the ruling class whose complex relations with the Party have caused major problems since 1949 when peace came to the land.

This problem exists in different forms in all modern societies, but seems least tractable where, as in China, the rulers have vested in themselves total control over all social activity, demand conformity to a single ideology which claims to be scientific (and therefore acceptable to intellectuals); and mistrust the higher intellectuals for their connections with the social groups whose dissolution was the very aim of the revolution.

The ultimate objective of the Party leaders was to turn the intellectuals into good communists, who would whole-heartedly devote their talents to the development of China on communist lines. (To the extent that this ideal was not reached, the need to supervise and coerce inevitably wastes some of this precious talent.) To achieve this, the Party kept the intellectuals at work on adequate salaries and set in train various procedures calculated to effect this transformation. Reading and discussing the daily press and basic documents of Marxism-Leninism constituted a steady process of general indoctrination. The gradual introduction of communist principles into working life followed. University teachers had to learn the Party's methods of criticism and self-criticism and accept the need both to adapt their courses to Marxist-Leninist principles and also to see the whole university system recast in order to meet the needs of a plan over which they had no control. These steady processes were intermittently reinforced by the stronger pressures of campaigns. In August 1949, for example, a U.S. State Department document, which could be read as implying that the United States Government regarded Chinese intellectuals as its potential allies, was used by the Party to whip up protestations of loyalty to itself and contempt for America. The war in Korea was used in a thousand ways to implant the idea that patriotism meant loyalty to the Chinese communist government and hostility to America. Various campaigns against distinguished intellectuals hostile to communism were used to isolate and destroy small recalcitrant minorities in order to scare the majority into conformity. They were characterized by exaggerated accusation, slander and false confessions.

This combination of pressures was superficially successful in that the great majority of intellectuals continued to work and became increasingly adept at behaving in a manner to conform with the Party's demands. It was a uniformity born of fear rather than devotion, and around 1956 the leaders showed signs of doubting their own policies. They admitted that some injustice had been done, and relaxed the pressures to conform. They probably realized that false loyalty and superficial conformity were common, and that they were still far from their ideal of an intellectual class genuinely devoted to communism. In 1957 this soft policy was carried a step farther when Mao invited the intellectuals to make a bigger contribution to the formulation of national policy and even to criticize the Party for its errors. This step upset the delicate balance of a totalitarian state. Although most intellectuals were cautious not to make any criticism liable to offend the leaders, a few were boldly rude and the very existence of this new liberal atmosphere started a dangerous ferment in the universities. Youth, it seemed, was less enamoured of communist controls than Mao and his colleagues had calculated.

The period of relaxation was abruptly ended. The Party reaffirmed the inviolability of its mandate, the few bolder critics were subjected to scorching public attack, and the rest of the intellectuals hastily reaffirmed their devotion to the Party leaders and the main lines of their policy.

The intellectuals seemed to lose still more ground during the Great Leap. To stimulate the enthusiasm of the masses, the Party deliberately belittled all forms of expertise. Later the intellectuals abased themselves in public processions to proclaim that they had 'handed their hearts to the Party'. Finally, 'voluntary' manual labour to purge away bourgeois tendencies served a punishment in all but name. In reality, however, the intellectuals' position showed a marked improvement. There was no return to the witch hunts and hard campaigns which had been frequent prior to 1956; new more liberal policies, though temporarily submerged in the Great Leap, remained on the statute book. When the Leap began to slump in 1960 the Party leaders again courted the intellectuals. In many spheres, decisions that require expert knowledge are now made by the experts, and these intellectuals, though they may not share the throne with the Party, stand close enough behind it to exercise some influence. Whether this uneasy and still recent situation will be maintained it is not possible to affirm. That same confidence which exists between political leaders and intellectuals in a democratic country cannot exist in China whose political leaders maltreated greatly their intellectuals so recently. However, were the Party to continue in its current lenient policies towards the intellectuals, confidence will grow up gradually and enable the intellectuals to serve better their country.

How, then, are we to sum up the history of the formation of a new ruling class in China? Beneath the legendary old guard, successive layers of human material have been thrown up from the lower levels of Chinese society in the course of military and political campaigns. The ruling class, now some seventeen million in numbers, is still expanding rapidly during the successive campaigns, but also shedding men unable to meet the new tests. It is a highly educated class, within the narrow and changing field of the current tasks as set by Mao and his group of colleagues in Peking; but its loyalty to these leaders has suffered with the failure of the Leap Forward and their inability to agree on one firm policy and stand united round Mao. The members of this class are used to control the whole sphere of operation or such part of the country they have in charge and to crush opposition with few exceptions. The intellectuals though outsiders are nevertheless an indispensable but lesser partner in the Party's enterprise of developing China. The Party maintains an uneasy balance between rigorous policies towards the intellectuals that would destroy their usefulness and a degree of relaxation that might weaken Party rule.

Rulers of a Closed Society

To what extent can such a ruling class be taken as a model? Our answer as stated at the outset, is twofold. First, will a political leader, who does not see his task in terms of totalitarian revolution, set about building a political army on Chinese communist lines? Scarcely. In a normal country the schools, industry, commerce, the civil service, the army, and the farms all have distinctive modes of life, their ruling classes which function without the continuous active intervention of a political army. These ruling classes are trained in their special problems and adjust themselves to their different modes of life. Political leaders do not assume that an élite reared for one task is equally effective for all others, still less that a single élite Party with complete control of all sectors of society is the key to development.

Second, can the ruling class created by the Chinese communist leaders effectively achieve the objects which they proclaim are China's only future? What has been done in education, industry, agriculture and other fields is told elsewhere in this book, but what is still unsolved is the organization of labour and brain in good teamwork. The Party's pressure is so hard and its controls so tight that the régime proceeds by jerks instead of moving smoothly as in an open society. China's advance on the path laid down by her communist leaders is much less efficient and far more hesitant than they dare admit even to themselves.

CHAPTER TWELVE

THE ROLE OF LEADERSHIP

DESMOND DONNELLY

The leadership of the Chinese Communist Party won its struggle for power in a vast, ramshackle country and achieved control over more than a fifth of mankind because it identified itself with the poverty-stricken lot of several hundred million Chinese peasants.

The Chinese communists, in their early years of power, governed with confidence born of practical experience and close association with the people. Then, as time passed, there was a change. Experience came to an end. New situations had to be faced for which there were no precedents. As in the history of all dictatorial leaderships that are not refreshed continually by new men and free contact with public opinion, authoritarian assertion, theory and dogma took the place of earlier and smoother processes. The cult of personality developed. Doubts, mistakes and recriminations followed each other. Even the competence to govern, in the fastest changing technological era in history, came into question. All this stemmed from the role that the Chinese communist leadership cast for itself. It is a small, very closely-knit group within whose intimate circle there is debate but whose view, once decided, is dictatorially imposed upon the whole Chinese nation.

Reduced to barest essentials, these are the main features of the story of the Party's leadership. In its vital and long period of struggle for power, and subsequent to it, the history of the Party's leadership, confronted by changing circumstances, may be divided into four periods:

1920–27: These were the fledgling years of coalition and infiltration, ending in disaster.

1927–49: The decisive period of revival and struggle; when total defeat was turned into complete victory.

1949–57: These were years of the heady honeymoon with the revolution and of gradual material progress even to the point at which Mao Tse-tung believed that a freer society might be introduced.

1957 on: Now came failure and disillusionment, especially amongst the intellectuals, followed by the grim struggle against reality.

1920–1927

The initial impact upon China of the Russian revolution was very limited. Events in European Russia appeared far away. Chinese opinion was more concerned at the time with President Wilson's Fourteen Points and the prospects that they might end foreign domination in China. Gradually, the significance of what had happened in the decisive days of 1917 filtered through to a limited number of Chinese intellectuals. As Mao Tse-tung put it later:

Before the October Revolution, the Chinese were not only unaware of Lenin and Stalin but did not even know of Marx and Engels. The salvoes of the October Revolution awoke us to Marxism-Leninism. The October Revolution helped the progressives of China and the whole world to adopt the proletarian world outlook as the instrument for studying a nation's destiny and considering anew their own problems. Follow the path of the Russians—that was their conclusion.—*On the People's Democratic Dictatorship* (1949)

The CCP's first great chance arose out of the circumstances prevailing in China at the time and the Sun Yat-sen–Joffe agreement of 1923. On the surface, the communist side made a number of concessions. Joffe agreed that 'the communistic order or even the Soviet system cannot actually be introduced into China' because the circumstances did not apply in the country. Sun Yat-sen refused to recognize the CCP as a unit affiliating to the Kuomintang, but considered it as a group of individuals who could constitute the Kuomintang's left wing. The action was known as the *Yung-Kung* policy (Let the communists join as individuals). For its part, the CCP leadership was faced with its first great opportunity—and test. At last it had the chance to impose its ideas, even if in limited form, upon a much larger and better established movement.

The objective of Borodin's mission and the CCP leadership was simple. They proposed to use the Kuomintang as the vehicle for the Chinese revolution. They had to strengthen it, at the same time always ensuring that the key posts went to CCP members. They persuaded Sun Yat-sen to reorganize the Kuomintang on Russian Communist Party lines, so that effective power was concentrated in the Party leadership at the top. Borodin even drafted the new Kuomintang constitution which was adopted at the KMT conference of January 1924. The CCP also introduced the system of political commissars and cadres in the army and administration—naturally using CCP members.

It was natural, in these circumstances of growing CCP influence, that difficulties should arise amongst the non-communist members of the KMT, many of whom had been attracted to Sun Yat-sen by his vigorous Chinese nationalism rather than his policies of social reform. Sun Yat-sen himself thought disingenuously that the Soviet Union was supporting his régime because it believed broadly in the reform policies for which he stood. Whilst he was alive he discouraged angry anti-communist moves on the right wing of the KMT. But his death—12 March 1925—created a new situation in which the internal stresses became public and the position of the CCP leaders much more vulnerable.

Although Chiang Kai-shek showed his anti-communist beliefs early, the CCP leaders continued to make common cause with him after Sun's death for two reasons. First, they probably still believed that they could best work towards 'a Chinese October' in this way. Secondly, even if they had differed from this view they had no option because Stalin had issued them instructions through the Comintern to co-operate with Chiang Kai-shek. Instead, the CCP leaders made determined efforts to strengthen their hold on the KMT. In Chiang's absence on his northern expedition, they forced the KMT Central Committee to adopt the principle of collective leadership with Chiang Kai-shek in a position subordinate to it. Again in Chiang's absence, they made the K\ headquarters of the régime to Wuhan where the\ were strong, whereas Chiang would have preferred

The truth was that in this brief period the C\ over-reached themselves. The result was the April 12\ The CCP's only answer was a series of ineffectual ьprisings, mainly in the cities, which Chiang put down easily.

There is an important parallel between the way in which the CCP sought to win power by infiltration and the famous 'salami' tactics that were deployed in Eastern Europe after 1945. The road that Sun Yat-sen first trod was to be followed by many unwary leaders of the European left. The essential condition, which prevailed in Prague in 1948 but which was missing in China in 1927, was the preponderance of Soviet military strength in the area. Chiang was able to strike back. Furthermore, the CCP was handicapped decisively by Stalin's misguided instructions from afar, forcing it 'to carry water on both shoulders'.

Ch'en Tu-hsiu, the General Secretary, who had been the loyal servant of Stalin's policies, took the major blame. He was indicted for his 'rightist opportunism'. After his final break with the CCP he wrote in a public message to all members:

I, who was not clear in perception or decisive in upholding my opinions, sincerely carried out the opportunist policy of the Communist International, and became the instrument of the narrow Stalinist faction. I could not save the Chinese Communist Party nor the revolution. . . .

In brief, the role of the CCP leadership up to 1927 was to act as the agent for the Comintern and the circumstances precluded success.

1927–1949

The most salutary commentary on the situation in which the CCP leadership found itself after the 1927 debacle, is the fact that the Sixth Party Congress was held in July 1928, in Moscow. Mao Tse-tung, a refugee from the defeated Hunan Autumn Crop uprising of the year before, was not present.

instead, he was carefully nursing the shattered remnants of his men in the remote mountain fortress of Chingkangshan, virtually cut off from the rest of the CCP leadership and from Moscow.

Mao himself had to carry the blame for the failure of the Autumn Crop uprising and of leading 'a rifle movement'. He had been removed from the Politbureau in a resolution adopted by the CCP Central Committee on 14 November 1927, after the uprising. Despite this, he was re-elected to the Central Committee at the 1928 Congress in his absence.

The rest of the CCP leadership remained in disarray. Its formal headquarters were in Shanghai where it could operate under the protection of the International Settlement. During the period following 1927, it had no less than six nominal leaders in eight years.

In the meantime, Mao had been joined at Chingkangshan by General Chu Teh after the uprising at Nanchang to establish what the two men called the Fourth Chinese Workers' and Peasants' Army, with Chu Teh as commander and Mao as political commissar. The gravamen of Mao's policy as described by Hu Ch'iao-mu, the official historian of the CCP, was that 'for the time being there was no way to win victory in the cities'. Instead, he proposed to 'encircle and subsequently to seize the cities that were occupied by counter-revolutionaries by means of armed, revolutionary rural districts'. Mao's tactics were briefly four:

> When the enemy advances, we retreat.
> When the enemy halts and encamps, we trouble him.
> When the enemy seeks to avoid battle, we attack.
> When the enemy retreats, we pursue.

His political and doctrinal problem was how to do this without coming into direct conflict with the policies of Stalin and the Comintern, who were supporting a series of disastrous uprisings in the cities. Mao did this by using the permissible expedient of claiming that he supported the rural proletariat in the remote area in which he had established himself.

The barren nature of the official CCP leadership's policy had gradually dawned upon the men in Shanghai. They decided in 1933 to transfer their headquarters to Mao Tse-tung's Chinese Soviet Republic. This decision was the start of Mao's dominance although it was to be acknowledged formally only later.

Mao's leadership became the accepted fact during the Long March of 1934–5 and was recognized at the Tsun-yi meeting of 1935. During this period Mao stood out as the great leader of men—for it is one thing to command forces when the tide of victory is flowing strongly, but it is another matter when defeat appears to be the only reward. The feat of covering 6,000 miles in 368 days, in the face of hazard and vicissitude, was so fantastic that there are few achievements in recorded history to compare with it—possibly only the great marches of Xenophon and Hannibal.

Mao's only possible rival, and equal in seniority in the party, Chang Kuo-t'ao, is said to have telegraphed his adherence to the Tsun-yi decisions, only to dispute them afterwards and be defeated at the Maoerhkai conference some seven months later. (Chang defected from the CCP in 1938, in his chagrin.)

The plight of the CCP at the end of the Long March was extremely poor; the men were exhausted, ragged and poorly equipped. In the circumstances, its leaders recognized that a continuing civil war would be greatly to their disadvantage. Therefore, at the Maoerhkai meeting, they decided also on a campaign for the Anti-Japanese National United Front, and called upon Chiang Kai-shek to stop the struggle 'against his own people'; they offered communist support for a drive against the Japanese invaders which Chiang had been neglecting in order to prosecute his campaign against the communists. At the very same time of the Maoerhkai meeting, the Seventh World Congress of the Comintern met to hear Dimitrov call for a global united front. There is evidence that the CCP had recently managed to resume radio contact with the Soviet Union.

The task of bringing about an anti-Japanese united front in China was not an easy one in view of all that had gone before. It was only after Chiang Kai-shek was 'kidnapped' by the 'Young Marshal', Chang Hsueh-liang, that the KMT's anti-communist campaigns were called off, the Red Army recognised as part of the Chinese Government forces and Mao's Yenan administration accepted as 'a special area government'. In return, the CCP nominally agreed to dissolve the Chinese Soviet Republic and to suspend its policies of land reform.

With its great experience in guerilla warfare, the CCP soon showed itself more adept than the KMT forces against the Japanese. Thereby, it assumed the lead in the anti-Japanese struggle behind the lines. Mao prepared carefully the policy of creating what he called 'liberated areas' under his administration. Where the KMT forces did not acknowledge CCP leadership, the Red Army's usual policy was to attack the KMT units and, after capturing them, incorporate them in its own forces.

In the new phase, disagreements between the KMT and CCP became most marked from 1940 onwards. Mao claimed, with justification, that the CCP was usually more active than the KMT in fighting the Japanese. Under cover of popular patriotism, the CCP made steady progress in far wider circles than those which might normally have been expected to support communism. Large numbers of the Chinese intelligentsia, bitterly humiliated by the success of the Japanese, were drawn into the communist cause.

Thus, besides identifying itself with the cause of the land-hungry Chinese peasantry, the CCP was following a national political cause that inevitably attracted public support. This skilful tactic was later successfully employed in Europe by Communist Parties in the resistance movements against the German occupation.

The increase of CCP forces during the war years and the extension of communist control in the so-called 'liberated areas' was most striking. The CCP had now reached the point of constituting a rival administration to Chiang's—a vital point when the Japanese armies in withdrawing were leaving vast empty areas to be taken over by the Chinese.

But Mao was in no position to take over the whole country. He took advantage of the situation only to the extent that he could assimilate territory, hold and control it effectively. It was a prudent policy. Therefore in his report to the CCP's Seventh Congress in Yenan in April 1945, Mao offered another form of coalition government with the KMT in which, whilst the administration would be shared, the political struggle would continue. In short, his offer was to desist from civil war but retain his right to continue the revolution.

President Truman, immediately after the war's end foresaw that there would inevitably be civil war between the KMT and CCP, unless steps were taken to avert it. From this arose the series of American initiatives culminating in the Marshall mission of 1946-7, which ended in failure because, by the end of 1947, Mao felt strong enough to drive out Chiang Kai-shek; and Chiang believed he could defeat the communists.

After an initial success of 1947, the tide of war turned against Chiang in 1948. The communists recaptured Yenan and, from Manchuria, where they had established their base after the Russian withdrawal, they marched south to overrun China. Their tactic was to infiltrate through the countryside with the support of the peasants, thus isolating the cities. The CCP leaders saw that their field commanders, administrative officers and occupation troops understood the absolute necessity of good behaviour and incorruptability. Amongst Mao's slogans that were put to music and sung by the Chinese Red Army, was the code of conduct:

> Be courteous and polite to people.
> Return all borrowed articles.
> Be honest in all transactions.
> Pay for all articles purchased.

To the Chinese in the KMT areas, it was an invading force the like of which China had never seen before.

Three issues faced by the CCP leaders stand out in the period of long struggle. First, they addressed themselves to the problems of contemporary China, and their programme—particularly their schemes for land reform—was always relevant. Secondly, they usually tempered their ambitions with prudence. Thus Mao, in particular, was ready to temporize if the CCP's strength did to match its task. Thirdly, they achieved victory largely without Soviet aid. There is little evidence of Soviet arms being supplied, even during the last phases of the civil war. Indeed Stalin and the Soviet Government, whatever their motives, broadly behaved correctly towards Chiang's administration and the Soviet Ambassador to China was the only diplomat representing a major power to follow the KMT Government in its flight as far south as Canton.

Disaster had been turned into complete victory.

1949–1957

When Mao stood on the balcony of the red Tien-an-men, surrounded by the leadership of the CCP in its hour of victory, it was a momentous event in Chinese history. There was dancing in the streets, and for many nights thereafter, until the chill winds of winter made it impracticable. Yet the fact that the dancing took place on the scene of what used to be a site for public executions in the days of Imperial China—and that some of it was spontaneous—indicates the national mood that met the communist leaders at the start of their régime.

The problems that confronted the CCP leaders in 1949 were daunting. The country's economy was stagnant; its industrial furniture—what there was of it—was antiquated. The administrative structure was as ramshackle as the industrial equipment. More than half the people were illiterate. Ignorance and prejudice had to be fought and destroyed in the long, hard struggle ahead. Dirt, poverty, hunger and disease were everywhere.

The leaders had one priceless asset, the goodwill of the people, who welcomed almost *any* new government, for as long as it was not corrupt and decadent, and brought peace.

Without wasting time, they nominated the new Government Council, the vice-premiers, ministers and other heads of government offices—this within a fortnight of their first proclamation. They were able to do so because (unlike most new governments) they had several advantages, and a substantial one over Lenin on the morrow of the Russian Revolution. Nearly all the inner core and the majority of the new administration were formed by people who had worked together for years in conditions of great hardship. They had shared common experiences such as the Shanghai purge, the Nanchang uprising, the Kiangsi Soviet, and the Long March itself. This gave the CCP leaders a bond of unity that is seldom granted to new régimes, whose members have followed diverse paths before coming together. Second, the CCP leadership had been acting as a provisional administration for years. Its members knew the realities of power and administration. They had been trained in the hardest of schools, in weighing policies that were possible as against more fanciful revolutionary dreams.

In the meantime throughout the country old scores were being paid off, particularly against landlords, money-lenders and compradores. It is estimated that, during these first months, something like 800,000 people were executed in one manner or another.

As to foreign relations, the first country to extend recognition to the People's Republic of China was the Soviet Union—the decision being taken the day after the proclamation of the new government. The other countries of the communist bloc followed in quick succession.

Mao had already made clear the CCP's position:

We must unite in a common struggle with the peoples of all countries and all nations who treat us as equals. This means allying ourselves with the Soviet Union, with every New Democratic country, and with the proletariat and broad masses in all countries. This means forming an international united front. . . . 'You are leaning to one side?' Exactly.

The twenty-eight years' experience of the Communist Party have taught us to lean to one side. . . . Sitting on the fence will not do, nor is there a third road.—*On the People's Democratic Dictatorship* (1949)

From this there could be no questioning where the priorities of the CCP leadership lay and why it was indifferent to the British gesture of recognition in 1950.

The Soviet monetary credit of 1950 gave the CCP leaders a small breathing space in the economy. The principal task was to step up agricultural production, China's main source of wealth. And Liu Shao-ch'i, reporting to the Second Session of the National Committee of the Chinese People's Political Consultation Conference on 14 June 1950, explained this policy. It was a clever and politic piece of reasoned exposition:

The basic reason for the aim of agrarian reform is different from the view that agrarian reform is only designed to relieve the poor people. The Communist Party has always been fighting for the interests of the labouring poor, but the viewpoints of communists have always been different from those of philanthropists. The results of agrarian reform are beneficial to the impoverished labouring peasants, helping them partly to solve their problem of poverty. But the basic aim of agrarian reform is not purely one of relieving the impoverished peasants. *It is designed to set free the rural productive forces from the shackles of the feudal land ownership system of the landlord class in order to develop agricultural production and thus pave the way for New China's industrialization.*

The careful planning of the land reform campaign showed that the CCP leaders had given it careful and intelligent thought.

The second big economic problem was the future policy towards industry, most of which was still in private hands. Mao Tse-tung had already laid down the general policy:

The New Democratic revolution will eliminate feudalism and monopoly capitalism. It will eliminate the landlord class and the bureaucratic bourgeoisie; but it will not eliminate capitalism in general, nor the petty and middle bourgeoisie. On account of the backwardness of the Chinese economy, it will be necessary to permit the existence, for a long time, even after national victory, of the capitalist economy represented by the broad petty bourgeoisie and middle bourgeoisie.—*The Turning Point in China* (1947)

In short, the leaders concentrated from the moment of assuming full power on a period of 'readjustment' in the 'transition to socialism'. And there were some parallels between the policy followed by Mao Tse-tung and Lenin's NEP of the early 1920's.

The CCP had been in power for less than a year when the war broke out in Korea on 25 June 1950. From the limited evidence available and by deduction, the invasion of South Korea by the North Koreans appeared to have been Soviet-inspired.

The Korean War soon posed grave problems of security—indeed of survival—as seen by the CCP leadership in Peking. To them, the intervention of the United States forces, acting on behalf of the United Nations, took on a very ominous turn when President Truman ordered the U.S. Seventh Fleet to secure the defence of Taiwan (Formosa). It looked like a military intervention in the civil war and when MacArthur's forces advanced northwards across the 38th Parallel to the accompaniment of a great deal of talk of an all-out war against communism, the alarm in Peking mounted.

Mao and his colleagues claimed that China was facing a repetition of the intervention by the Western Powers in the Russian Revolution and they reacted accordingly.

The national feeling that had accompanied establishment of the new régime was deepened in the patriotic upsurge engendered by the Korean War. The CCP leaders were quick to take advantage of it in their policies for production drives, and in their skilful propaganda campaigns against corruption. Indeed, it was this combination of two successive waves of national support that enabled Mao to overcome the early inertia of the country and also to meet the demands of the Korean campaign.

In 1954–5, there occurred the first major split in the CCP leadership after victory. Kao Kang, who had been the local communist leader in northern Shensi, to which Mao's forces made their way after the Long March, and who was later in charge of Manchuria, was accused of separatist aims and of attempting to set up an independent Manchurian state. Kao, who was then the chairman of the State Planning Commission, and its vice-chairman, Jao Shu-shih, were both stripped of their Party offices. Five governors and many party functionaries in the lower echelons were deposed in the purge.

There is no evidence that Kao was thinking in terms of deposing Mao. It is much more likely that he hoped to win his points within the leadership for greater political and economic decentralization in defeating Liu Shao-ch'i and Chou En-lai within the Party councils. It is significant that throughout the Kao Kang dispute Mao virtually played no public part and the chief accuser of Kao was Liu Shao-ch'i. Whilst the dispute was presented in personalized terms, there were undoubtedly deeper policy issues that crystallized around Kao Kang, whose suicide was announced in 1955.

The second stage of the economic programme of socialization of industry and collectivization of agriculture moved with much greater speed in 1953–5 than was the case with the earlier land-reform movement. It was due partly to the more effective control of the Central Government. But a deeper reason was that the CCP leadership was now moving out of the realm of its practical experience and relying more on Marxist theory, which it believed to be infallible.

For example, Chou En-lai addressing the National People's Congress, in September 1954, said that half the 110 million peasant households in the country would be brought into co-operatives by 1957, the end of the first Five-Year Plan. A year later, on 31 July 1955, Mao Tse-tung suddenly pressed for greater speed in his statement on the *Question of Agricultural Co-operation*. There must have been a sharp debate within the Party before Mao placed himself on the left and embarked upon the accelerated programme. He said as much in his directive when referring to members of the Central Committee who had disagreed.

It was at this point that Khrushchev delivered his denunciation of Stalin to the Twentieth Congress of the Communist Party of the Soviet Union, which was followed by the Polish and Hungarian revolutions and a turmoil throughout world communism. A new era in the problems facing the CCP leadership was beginning.

1957 Onwards

The reaction of Mao Tse-tung and the Party leaders to the events of 1956 in Poland and Hungary was one of alarm. Externally, they were quite ready to use the situation to strengthen their right to doctrinal leadership. Indeed, the Chinese attitude in the Polish revolt was the forerunner of Mao Tse-tung's overt challenge to Khrushchev's policies and the Soviet leadership of the communist bloc. Internally, however, Mao considered that the time had come for an easement of political dictatorship, provided always that the basic fabric of the communist state was not brought into question. This is the explanation for the episode that came to be known as the 'Hundred Flowers' period. That Mao felt completely secure in his position was made clear in his speech *On the correct handling of contradictions among the People*, on 27 February 1957, at the 11th Session of the Supreme State Conference:

The Communist Party is strong and its prestige stands high. Although there are defects and mistakes in our work, every fair-minded person can see that we are loyal to the people, that we are both determined and able to build up our country together with the people and that we have achieved great successes and will achieve greater ones. The vast majority of the bourgeoisie and intellectuals from the old society are patriotic; they are willing to serve their flourishing socialist motherland and they know that if they turn away from the socialist cause and the working people led by the Communist Party, they will have no one to rely on and no bright future to look forward to.

His words are a clear illustration of how far eight years of power can isolate any leader from the mood of the people. The consequence was disillusionment at the centre and angry bewilderment at local levels where lesser Party officials were confronted by the denunciations of people who 'blossomed'. The CCP leaders showed their flexibility—unusual amongst authoritarian rulers—in the way in which the 'Hundred Flowers' policy was placed in reverse and the situation actually capitalized to strengthen the régime by holding up the 'rightists' as examples to be avoided. Undaunted, the leaders did not take to excessive caution, for in 1958 Mao announced the communes policy and the Great Leap Forward, aimed at the large-scale industrialization of China by the end of the 1960's.

Nevertheless, the 'Hundred Flowers' episode was symptomatic. The gulf, which was growing between the CCP leadership and reality, appeared again—this time in the field of economics—when exaggerated reports of production figures led to a premature announcement that the grain crop had risen from 185 million tons in 1957 to 375 million tons in 1958. The humiliation Mao suffered with the failure of his 'Hundred Flowers' was now Chou En-lai's to suffer in announcing the revised figure of 250 millon tons of grain. Even these figures were probably exaggerated—for how else can the subsequent severe food shortages be explained. Two hundred million tons is probably the more accurate estimate.

A third example of the growing divergence between the leadership's expectations and realities is the strange affair of the 'backyard steel furnaces'. Whereas people with any common sense would know that untutored workers, operating with primitive techniques, were unlikely to make steel in large quantities—and if they did so it would be of poor quality— Mao and his colleagues thought otherwise and were proved wrong.

The inevitable result was that the Great Leap Forward and its aims were buried finally by the policy of 'consolidation' at the Ninth plenary session of the CCP Central Committee in January 1961. A similar miscalculation of the practical caused a cutback in the communes policy, which was designed as an expedient for mobilizing labour effectively rather than as a doctrinal conception in itself as presented by the Party. The detailed planning of the tactics to be followed, coupled by a playing down of the difficulties of the grand strategy—the basis of earlier successes—were markedly absent.

The confidence and sense of direction that had characterized the CCP's policy ever since Mao Tse-tung had assumed the leadership in 1935 was now no longer. Outwardly the leadership retained most of its cohesion. Mao's personal position was still unassailable, although, in 1959, he divested himself of the title of Chairman of the People's Republic to concentrate on Party affairs. But the breaks, in public, which in earlier times had been confined to such rare cases as Chang Kuo-t'ao in 1938, and Kao Kang in 1954, have become more numerous.

Whereas Chang Kuo-t'ao's breach with Mao can be explained largely by personal rivalry between two men of similar seniority, there was an equally simple explanation of Kao Kang's defection. Kao had only come into the leadership at a high level at the end of the Long March and had never shared the earlier experiences of vicissitude that bound together the others. To that extent, he was naturally more independent in his outlook.

Policy differences now appeared. Despite Mao's reluctance to permit any public conflicts, open breaches took place. First, there was the growth of the two factions within the leadership, the radical leftists and the moderate rightists. It is believed that the moderates included many of the men with practical day-to-day responsibility for government, headed by Chou En-lai, Li Fu-ch'un, Teng Tzu-hui, Ch'en Yün and Po I-po. Certainly their duties were gravely prejudiced by Mao's speech on the *Correct Handling of Contradictions*, and for some weeks their authority in the country was in question. Later, the Great Leap Forward and the communes added enormously to their administrative burdens, to the point that the government machine broke down on occasion. On the radical left, there were the theoreticians, led by Liu Shao-ch'i, Teng Hsiao-p'ing, T'an Chen-lin, Lu Ting-i and Ch'en Po-ta. Mao's tactic was usually to await the outcome of the internal Party debate and to place himself at the head of the radical leftists at the decisive moment. Thus he played his part, first in speeding up collectivization in 1955, and then in demanding faster economic progress in 1956. Again, he was in the van of the Great Leap Forward campaign in 1958.

The first consequence of these internal alignments was the temporary replacement of Teng Tzu-hui as the CCP's chief spokesmen on agricultural matters during the collectivization drive; and later the position of Po I-po was in question for a while. The most important open breach came however in Ch'en Yün's opposition to the Great Leap Forward and his public disgrace when he ceased active participation in affairs for several months—details of the dispute are still not clear. He remains formally a member of the Politbureau, as Mao has always shown himself to be reluctant to make a final break because it contradicts the benevolent father figure, which he cultivates so carefully.

A complete break did come, however, in the cases in 1959 of P'eng Te-huai, the minister of Defence, and Chang Wen-t'ien, the senior vice-minister of Foreign Affairs. Both men are strongly suspected to have sided with the Soviet Union, first in the doctrinal divergences between the Soviet Communist Party and CCP on the communes policy and also in the wider Sino-Soviet dispute that also came into the open in 1958. P'eng Te-huai in his capacity as minister of Defence would have been fully aware of China's dependence on Soviet military strength and the practical dangers inherent in Mao's belligerent rejection of the coexistence concept. Chang Wen-t'ien was educated in the Soviet Union, active in Manchuria in 1945–50 from the period of the Soviet military occupation onwards, and Ambassador to Moscow from 1951 to 1955. These men were treated more severely in their dismissals than the moderate rightists in internal affairs because, from the Chinese communist point of view, their greater crime was siding with another country's policy. More recently Yang Hsien-chen has been attacked. He is a member of the Central Committee and was head of the Higher Party School until 1959. This is the first public attack since the purge of 'rightists' in 1957/1958. Yang has been rebuked for expressing revisionist views at the Higher Party School, as recently as April 1964. He has been denounced as a renegade who must be removed from any position of responsibility.

The Sino-Soviet dispute is—in foreign affairs—the most recent disregard of reality by the Chinese leaders, in the same way as their most ambitious economic plans have been in internal affairs. The CCP leadership (as it left behind its practical military experience of the pre-1949 period and the 'limited' war in Korea) has resorted more and more to political theory in its attitudes to competitive coexistence. It has dogmatized, not reasoned. It has taken little or no note of the impact of technology on the pattern of world struggle, and still adheres to outdated beliefs regarding the patterns and intentions of Western society. Thus, in its approach to world politics, the CCP leadership is now in the same false posture that the Great Leap created in the economy.

The Final Question

A final question arises: Can the CCP leadership reverse its present attitudes and return to the pragmatic flexibility of its earlier years? The answer is in the structure of Chinese Communist government and the role cast for itself by the leadership. The system is a dictatorship. Mao's whole policy has been to centralize power within the Party leadership and he has made considerable efforts—broadly with success—to retain its cohesion at the top. When CCP leadership spoke of democratic centralism, it meant the concentration of power in the Politbureau, not in the constitutional machine to which it pays lip-service. All the apparatus of the authoritarian state, the secret police, the direction of justice and the use of force, uphold the central power. The leadership may have set out with the intention of retaining support in the country as a whole but it has alienated in turn and cut itself off from whole classes of the people. The disillusionment of the peasants, created by the collectivization drive, is matched amongst the intellectuals in the 'Hundred Flowers' affair. And Government's harsh economic policies in industry have not fulfilled the early expectations of the urban populations.

The leadership's present position is both its strength and its greatest weakness. Its cohesion at top level has been a great asset in the past in winning power and deciding policies. Its very cohesion has led to its increasing remoteness from the people it governs. Its reluctance to introduce new personnel at the top has come to the point that it is destroying the leadership's earlier effectiveness. These are the classic diseases of dictatorship, leading to their eventual downfall.

History's judgment of Mao Tse-tung and his colleagues is almost certain to be that they began as one of the most effective and determined groups of men who set out to shape the pattern of affairs in history. But an objective view will also decide that they too have fallen victim to the law of politics—as fundamental as Newton's law of gravity—that whereas authoritarianism is an effective practice in the short run, in the end it is self-defeating. This lesson has to be learned anew by each generation of every nation.

BIBLIOGRAPHY

Beloff, Max, *Soviet Policy in the Far East*. London 1953.
China Quarterly edited by Roderick MacFarquhar, London.
Clark, Gerald, *Impatient Giant*. London 1960.
Chiang Kai-shek, *China's Destiny*. New York 1947.
Davidson-Houston, J. V., *Russia and China*. London 1960.
Donnelly, Desmond, *The March Wind*. London 1959.
Fitzgerald, C. P., *Revolution in China*. London 1952.
——*Flood Tide in China*. London 1958.
Freemantle, Anne, *Mao Tse-tung: An Anthology of his Writings*. New York 1962.
Feis, Herbert, *The China Tangle*. New York 1953.
Hu Ch'iao-mu, *Thirty Years of the Communist Party of China*. Peking 1951.
Hu Hua, *History of the Chinese New Democratic Revolution*. Canton 1951.
Liu Shao-ch'i, *On the Party*. Peking 1950.
——*On the Inner Party Struggle*. Peking, undated.
MacFarquhar, Roderick, *The Hundred Flowers*. London 1960.
Mao Tse-tung, *Selected Works*, Vols I-IV. Peking 1961.
Rostow, W. W., *The Prospects for Communist China*. New York 1954.
Shabab, Theodore, *China's Changing Map*. New York 1956.
Snow, Edgar, *Red Star Over China*. London 1937.
Tang, Peter S. H., *Communist China Today*. New York 1957.
Walker, R. L., *China under Communism*. New York 1955.

THE CHINESE MODEL AND THE DEVELOPING COUNTRIES

GEOFFREY HUDSON

It is not the task of the concluding chapter of this symposium to summarize what has been said in the previous sections. It seems appropriate, instead, to direct the attention of the reader once more to some of the principal features of the Chinese scene in so far as they are relevant to other countries seeking solutions of their problems of political development, economic growth, and social change.

The Editor

The great paradox of Marxism in the twentieth century has been the contrast between its theory of socialist revolution as the climax of industrial capitalist development and the restriction of its practical political success to societies of relatively backward, and predominantly agrarian, economy. In classical Marxist doctrine proletarian revolution and the transition from capitalism to socialism is predetermined by the development of the capitalist economy which, it is claimed, through the expansion of industry, at once urbanizes and reduces to the level of wage slaves an increasing majority of the population. The further capitalist industry advances through capital investment and the application of scientific technology, the greater becomes the contradiction—so Marxist theory maintains—between the ever-dwindling numbers of the owners of property and the ever-increasing numbers of the disinherited. The explosion due to aggravated tension between the rich few and the poor many was thus expected to occur first in one of the wealthiest and most highly industrialized societies. It was assumed that in such a society the bourgeois social revolution would have been completed, that feudal relations in agriculture would have been eliminated, that modern industry would be a going concern and that the basic problem of feeding the population, whether from home agriculture or foreign trade, would have been solved.

The first revolution under Marxist leadership nevertheless took place, not in one of the most highly industrialized countries, but in one which, although it ranked as one of the Great Powers of Europe, was economically the most backward of the nations in that category. When after the Second World War, Communist Party rule was extended to countries besides Russia, the restriction of real revolutionary impetus to economically backward regions was even more striking. The advances of communism in Eastern Europe were for the most part due to the military intervention of the Soviet armed forces or to the threat of it; the only area in which communism showed inherent power of its own was in South-western Yugoslavia, Albania and Northern Greece—a zone of rural poverty virtually devoid of modern industry. On the other side of the Soviet Union, communism triumphed in China, conquering the towns from rural strongholds in which it had established itself through years of civil war and Japanese invasion.

In China the Marxist cause gained a country much less industrialized in 1949 than Russia had been in 1917. The great bulk of the population consisted of cultivators living by subsistence agriculture, and the only important centres of modern industry had been hitherto under foreign control. Russia, although lagging behind Western Europe economically, had been a great imperial power, even before the First World War. China, by contrast, had remained between the wars 'semi-colonial', with extraterritorial rights for foreigners and foreign-administered leased territories, and in 1945 only got rid of Japanese rule in Manchuria at the price of new checks on Chinese sovereignty extorted by the Soviet Union.

The Choice before the Developing Countries

Today the countries of Asia, Africa and Latin America which are regarded by Peking as ripe for revolution are, like China, all predominantly agrarian societies, many of them ex-colonial with modest or negligible industrial development, dependent on foreign capital or financial and technical aid for any progress they hope to make. Since in the advanced industrialized countries of Western Europe and North America communism has no prospect of achieving a violent seizure of power by the classic methods of revolutionary insurrection, it has been reduced to renouncing the once essential doctrine of inevitable civil war and to trying to build up a reputation as a respectable democratic force. Since the Twentieth Congress, the 'revisionism' of Soviet ideology, apart from emphasizing the possibility of avoiding international war, has been part of an attempt to revive the communist movement within the Western democracies on a basis of practical politics no longer dependent on the fading hopes of the appearance of a new Lenin. This adaptation of Russian communist theory to conditions confronting the communist cause in the industrial West reflects the preoccupations of the Soviet Union at the present day as both a highly industrialized and a primarily European power.

In most of the 'underdeveloped' countries, on the other hand, mass poverty and illiteracy, scarcity of capital, the absence of a strong middle class, and the lack of generally valued or accepted political institutions offer prospects for the kind of revolutionary upheavals which Lenin and Mao Tse-tung exploited in seizing political power and setting up communist régimes. Recent colonial or semi-colonial subjection to Western powers renders the historical experience of the newly emerging countries more analogous to that of China than to that of Russia. In any event, the industrial break-through of the last ten years has put Russia today very much further beyond the Russia of the Tsars than Mao's China is beyond the China of Chiang Kai-shek.

The political forces in underdeveloped countries, which aim at changing the existing system, usually are eager for rapid development. They often are dismayed by the great gulf between their own situation and that in nations which have accomplished their break-through into modernity over a long span of time. Unable to view the example of the advanced countries as relevant to themselves and their immediate circumstances in practical terms, these leaders often tend to see as the only choice for their aspiration that between the Russian and Chinese models. For sheer power and wealth, the Russian model is obviously the more impressive of the two: Russia's huge industrial plants are immensely exciting to idealists of the new age obsessed with visions of swift economic growth, and the Russians can provide financial and technical assistance on a scale impossible for the Chinese. But Russia shares to a great extent with the industrial countries of the West the disadvantage of being remote from the conditions and problems which confront underdeveloped societies.

The revolutionary leaders of emerging countries may be profoundly impressed by a visit to, say, Magnitogorsk, but what they want to know is, first, how to establish a 'people's government' in power, and, second, how to take appropriate steps in 'building socialism'. In order to learn from the Soviet experience how to make a revolution they would have to go back to 1917. Even then the model would be difficult to imitate. Few newly emerging countries today have in their capital cities an industrial proletariat as strong as that of St. Petersburg in 1917, and none can count on the special circumstance of a prolonged and unpopular foreign war which causes troops to turn against their officers.

In this situation the example of China may appear more generally applicable. A revolution which grows to maturity in the countryside and only conquers the cities after it has worn down the forces of the central government by guerilla warfare may be thought suitable in any country which has extensive jungles or mountain areas, much agrarian discontent, and an irresolute, incompetent or corrupt administration. The Chinese model was successfully copied by Castro in Cuba and it is being followed by the Vietcong in South Vietnam and by Mulele in the Congo. There may well be other cases in future where it will appeal to the leaders of revolutionary forces.

The Language of Revolution

The prestige of the Chinese revolutionary model is enhanced by the fact that, since the divergence of foreign policies between Moscow and Peking, China has been the champion of revolutionary movements in Asia, Africa and Latin America, while Russia has—though not altogether consistently—subordinated support for such developments to the purposes of 'peaceful coexistence' with the United States. The stirring language of revolution spoken in Peking tends to appeal more strongly to young men in a hurry than the more cautious avuncular advice from Moscow.

The effect of the difference in terms of potential backing for a revolution is not so great as might be supposed from the verbal contrasts. Outside the immediate neighbourhood of China's frontiers, the Chinese have virtually no capacity for military intervention anywhere. In Panama or the Congo they can bark, but they cannot bite. Russia's power, on the other hand, is such that biting is a practical proposition in any international crisis arising out of a revolution anywhere, but it might be fatal for all those involved. Since Russia would have no good excuse for not following up barking with biting in a crisis, its leaders have to be more careful about their barking than the Chinese. Paradoxically, therefore, Russia is placed at a disadvantage in relation to China by her immensely greater armed power. As long as China's capacity to help is not put to the test, Mao Tse-tung can play the role of leader of world revolution which, he maintains, Khrushchev abdicated.

Communists and their supporters in developing countries may find more in the Chinese than in the Russian experience, as the Chinese communist idea of manpower as a source of capital seems better suited to meet the needs of poverty-stricken societies, whose leaders are unwilling to become too dependent on foreign aid. The Russians under Stalin followed lines of capitalist development in so far as they thought of industrial growth as essentially urban and necessarily involving the transfer of population from the countryside to the towns. The Chinese communists, after coming to power, at first sought to follow the same road; very large complexes of urban industry and new cities were planned. But China had even less margin for capital accumulation than Russia had had in the 'thirties', and less capacity to obtain foreign exchange by exports.

When, therefore, Russian aid to China fell short of expectations, and serious bottlenecks developed in the economy towards the end of 1957, the Chinese leadership fell back on the idea of making use of the great reserve of under-employed manpower available in the countryside. To industrialize on the cheap was the basic purpose behind the communes and the hortatory propaganda of the Great Leap Forward. The communes were to organize not only agriculture, but also all kinds of local industries as well as the building of roads, canals and irrigation dams. Precedents for such rural enterprises were supplied by the years of the guerilla war, when the communist armed forces had supplied themselves largely from small-scale industrial production in the villages.

The commune system with its 'backyard steel' made by peasants appeared to magnify the importance of the countryside in relation to the towns, and indeed would have done so if the non-agricultural activities had not been promoted at the expense of agriculture. But in fact Chinese agricultural production suffered a disastrous setback in the Great Leap Forward, and the whole industrial programme was slowed down by the failure of the sector on which the feeding of the population depended. Natural calamities were blamed for the decline in food production, and indeed they occurred—as they always have done at frequent intervals in a country subject to such great climatic hazards as China—but the crisis was largely man-made.

Peking had claimed, erroneously, that the 'communist' economy provided immunity from the famines of the past. There was plenty of evidence that agriculture suffered from lack of incentives for the peasants under the commune system and from priorities for non-agricultural tasks which transformed under-employment in the villages into shortages of labour on the land at critical times of the agricultural year. The Great Leap Forward, after a spectacular start, petered out in a humiliating anticlimax, with Peking buying grain abroad to assure minimum rations for the people, new factories standing idle because of non-delivery of raw materials, and engineering plants rejecting backyard steel because of its low quality.

Soon after the collapse of Chinese plans for industry on account of failure in agriculture, the Soviet Union ran into serious economic trouble due to agricultural deficiencies and was reduced to purchasing wheat from the United States. The fact that in both China and Russia plans for agriculture came to grief in spite of boastful claims of expansion indicates the most fundamental defect of communism as an economic system—its inability to cope with problems of rural productivity. This is due to the basic attitude of Marxism towards the countryside. Marxism is the product of an urban intelligentsia and it is characterized by an inherent dislike and distrust of the cultivator.

Rural Obstacle to Communist Rule

When Marx spoke of 'rural idiocy' he expressed exactly his thought on the subject. Marxism preaches that all progress comes from the towns; the countryside is the stronghold of conservatism and outmoded custom. The desire of the cultivator to own his land and to dispose of his produce in his own way is considered an obstacle to communist rule. The ideal for agriculture is the 'grain factory' in which the production of crops will be organized with wage-earning labour on industrial lines. Pending the attainment of this goal, however, cultivators may be politically helpful if their antagonism to landlords and officials can be utilized so as to make them allies of the communist revolutionary avant-garde.

In China the 'ruralization' of the revolution was its outstanding feature during the period of armed struggle. Communist power was maintained regionally for years with rural support, and it gave rise to the myth, once very widespread, that the Chinese communists were merely 'agrarian reformers'. Yet neither in Russia nor in China did convinced Marxist-Leninists ever have any sympathy for the aspirations of the peasantry. Here then lies a lesson worth studying before deciding on the relation of town and country or industry and agriculture in any plans of development anywhere.

In China, as in Russia, the communist leadership was dedicated to high-speed industrialization and was ready to sacrifice everything else to it. The excessive concentration on industry, however, proved to be self-defeating, for industrialization had to be slowed down when agriculture failed to do what was required of it. The Chinese communists have recently shown a certain realism in drawing conclusions from this experience. Steel is no longer 'the leading link'. The communist order of priority, i.e. heavy industry, light industry, agriculture, has been reversed for the time being, so as to give the first priority to agriculture, and to yield to the compelling necessity of feeding a population of over 600 million people on the limited returns of a subsistence economy. However, this change of priorities cannot be regarded as anything but a temporary expedient. The priority for agriculture which has been forced on the Chinese communists runs counter to their strongest convictions and desires. It means that industrialization proceeds much more slowly than was intended, and that the communists' claim to have found a short cut to an advanced industrial society had to be temporarily abandoned.

The lessons of the Chinese experience are of supreme importance to developing countries, where the overriding purpose of the politically conscious and educated classes is rapid industrialization. Communists commend themselves as providing short cuts to this end. A single-party state and nationalization of economic enterprises, it is argued, will make it possible to achieve industrialization quickly, and the sacrifice of political and civil liberties is presented as only a small price to pay for the greater speed of development. It is assumed that the short cut is possible and that Russia and China have shown it to be so. But it is just these assumptions which need to be scrutinized. The economic distortion involved in communist priorities exacts its price sooner or later, and the less developed the society, the heavier the price is likely to be.

In terms of balanced all-round economic development and human welfare the claims of communism's superior speed of growth are fallacious, at any rate if they are compared not with the stagnation of a decaying traditional order, but with what can be accomplished by a reasonably free society aiming at balanced, orderly development of all sectors of the economy with the aid of intelligently directed technical assistance from abroad.

Pattern of Social Change

The social cost of the communist solution is even greater than that caused by economic dislocation. It is in fact merely another facet of one and the same phenomenon, the break with the past by exclusively violent processes. There is more than one country in Asia, Africa and Latin America where social change is likely to take violent forms in the absence of gradual reforms long overdue. Young revolutionary leaders are therefore likely to study with great interest the Chinese pattern as the most recent, if not the most successful case of change of traditional social values.

Modernization in developing countries produces almost invariably an alienation of the educated class, including both the opinion-forming intellectuals and the policy-forming officials, from the majority of the population. In traditional society the chief, landlord, elder and local magnate, however oppressive, are culturally akin to the people among whom they live. As the *raison d'être* of their existence disappears, there is no longer any intermediate element between the mass of the people and the new town-based ruling groups of merchants and manufacturers, politicians and officials of central and regional governments. The breaking-up of traditional society in face of the growing strength of new social forces is a painful process in the best of circumstances. Every country that moves from the Middle Ages to modern times is bound to experience it. Communist China is by no means alone in this respect. What makes it unique is the thoroughness with which traditional loyalties have been broken and men's minds have been conditioned on the most massive scale to accept nothing but the one and only loyalty created and approved by the Party in power.

Nothing quite like this happened in the first years following the Bolshevik revolution. The social pattern of Tsarist Russia had undergone considerably more change than that of China in the decades following the Taiping rebellion (1850–1864), the last occasion on which the old order was defended successfully against the rising forces demanding a new social order. Later on Sun Yat-sen insisted on constitutional democracy as the political objective of the revolution whose spiritual father he was. He underestimated, however, the handicap which the lack of new social forces presented to his attempt at political change. The years following the revolution of 1911, which ended almost three hundred years of Manchu rule, and the setting-up of the Republic in 1912 did not suffice to create middle and working classes like those on which Lenin could draw in preparing and winning his revolution against the established order.

While the Moscow-trained communists failed to understand the pecularities of the Chinese situation, Mao Tse-tung set out systematically to base himself on the largest sector of society in his attempt at changing the social structure of the country. The cultivators were to become his revolutionary tools and land reform his means of winning them over. In his work *On New Democracy* (1940) he gave notice that in the absence of an industrial proletariat the Chinese revolution would be led by the joint dictatorship of several revolutionary classes, i.e. the communist cadres and the cultivators. After that there could be no longer any question of a return to Lenin's revolutionary pattern of 1917.

Land reform provided the opportunity to affix a class label to every member of the rural community, and 'speak bitterness' meetings provided the public occasions at which to assault established loyalties. Brain washing has become known mainly as a tool used among members of foreign armed forces taken prisoner during war. In fact, it is the technique which has been applied to a whole nation, the largest on earth. Once existing loyalties had been destroyed, the new paternalism of the Party could be expected to be accepted as the only substitute in sight. Only thus can be explained the temporary success of this greatest and most ruthless experiment of social engineering in modern times. When the first awakening occurred and it found expression in the period of the 'Hundred Flowers', new forms of persuasion were employed which drew on the experience gathered in the course of accusation meetings, 'anti-campaigns' and brain-washing proceedings.

By comparison with these nation-wide operations, the handling of such organized bodies as 'democratic parties' and religious groups was a relatively trifling affair. Powerful radio transmitters, verbose news agencies and other mass media, together with the more conventional organs of education, could be trusted to secure a degree of national conformity probably never achieved before by any revolutionary régime. The approach that led to success at home was, not unnaturally, assumed to be applicable abroad; hence the rejection as 'bourgeois nationalist' of patriotic movements in developing countries that aim at political and social change whilst preserving indigenous cultural values instead of disrupting all existing loyalties à la chinoise.

The concept is so exclusively Chinese that here lies one of the roots of the complete disregard for not only India's national aspirations but also Russia's approach to the question of communist world domination by means of 'peaceful coexistence'. While the Chinese pattern will unquestionably have a strong appeal in certain revolutionary situations, it is likely to antagonize the more experienced and sophisticated political leaders of newly emerging countries by reason of its uncompromising attitude towards traditional loyalties at home and national aspirations abroad, both of which will be found essential in the formation of new nation states.

Politics Take Command

Last, but not least, there is the political aspect of the Chinese model. Mao himself once recalled that before the Bolshevik revolution the Chinese people were not only unaware of Lenin and Stalin, but they did not even know of Marx and Engels. Yet, from a handful of fervent believers in the correctness of Marxism as a working concept for revolutionary change, the Chinese Communist Party grew within the first decade following the Russian October revolution to almost sixty thousand. Twenty years later it had more than a million active members, and it was ready to seize power over one-fifth of the world's population.

In the interval, the Party had grown, through internal strife and after near-defeat, from a group of revolutionaries following the path of the Soviet leadership to an independent national Communist Party, though organized in all essentials on the Soviet pattern of strict 'democratic centralism'. It had gained political, military and administrative experience in many years of guerilla warfare, first against the forces of the Kuomintung and later in co-operation with them against the Japanese invasion. It had governed rural areas, first in the Southwest and later in the Northwest of the country, living off the land among cultivators and enrolling them into the ranks of the Party. It had gained support from intellectuals dissatisfied with the Kuomintang's performance in the fight against the Japanese armies, and it had incorporated large sections of the armed forces of the KMT after penetrating or defeating them.

When faced, after victory, with the different challenge of peace-time development, the team of political leaders and the Party which served them seemed less successful in directing the nation towards prosperity. The concept of total control over all activities, inescapable in war and civil war, revealed its inherent weakness when put to the test of turning a backward agrarian community in a short space of time into a modern industrial society.

The intellectuals, forced to conform to a pattern of monolithic political power, showed signs of restlessness when they were given half a chance to express themselves. Factions of 'rightists' and 'leftists' formed even within the Party, renowned for its internal unity, on such divergent issues as the priority of industry over agriculture during the period of the Great Leap Forward, or the supremacy of revolutionary upheaval over 'peaceful coexistence' in the doctrinal exchanges of the Sino-Soviet dispute.

It is impossible to anticipate the means by which a balance can be maintained between policies of central control which may be self-defeating and measures of relaxation that might threaten the very existence of the Party. What does seem certain is that it will remain a very uneasy balance, and that the outcome of the struggle of conflicting forces will be a long way from the communist millennium that was featured as a target within easy reach when the Great Leap Forward was brought into being.

There is no free interchange of views between rulers and ruled in China today. Concentration of power in the hands of the Politbureau takes the place of delegation of power by constitutional means. There is thus inherent in the communist system of China both strength and weakness, cohesion of leadership side by side with an unwillingness, characteristic of all authoritarian régimes, to abdicate the leadership of the nation to a political alternative ready to accept responsibility when the passion of the Party in power has been spent.

Nothing that has so far been achieved by the communist régime in China indicates that Marxism-Leninism provides a key whereby the necessary consequences of backwardness can miraculously be avoided. China has set no example to the developing countries of the world which should convert intelligent observers to the communist faith by the evidence of success. The mystique of Maoism will no doubt continue to operate and sustain guerilla fighters in jungle lairs; but by the criterion of its performance Communist China is not in a position to match, let alone outbid other alternatives.

The problems in that greater part of the world which has been left behind in the march of modern development are of fundamental importance for our age; they require for their solution drastic criticism of theoretical assumptions as well as procedures of trial and error to meet conditions which are without precedent in history. But for these enquiries and experiments freedom of thought and political opposition are essential. Where leaders are irremovable and failures, or responsibilities for them, can be concealed by political censorship, the consequences of error tend to be greatly magnified and perpetuated.

Chinese communism clearly has not produced a body of absolute knowledge capable of predictable results which could possibly justify a totalitarian system. It has furnished no workable solution to the problem of developing retarded nations.

LIST OF CONTRIBUTORS

G. BARRASS is assistant editor of *The China Quarterly;* formerly on the staff of *The Economist* as a contributor on *Far Eastern Affairs.*

J. BUSBY has been a student of contemporary Chinese affairs since the end of the last war. He spent a number of years in China both before and after the 1949 revolution and has contributed articles to professional journals, in England and elsewhere.

D. DONNELLY is Member of Parliament for Pembroke. He has travelled extensively. Following several tours of Eastern Europe, Soviet Russia and the mainland of China, he wrote *The March Wind* (Explorations behind the Iron Curtain). He is a regular contributor to British journals and newspapers.

V. FUNNELL is with the Chinese Section of the British Broadcasting Corporation. He was born in Szechwan, West China, and he lived also in Shanghai and in Shantung province. He was for some years with the New Zealand Department of External Affairs. He is engaged in a study of social problems in China at the London School of Economics.

A. M. HALPERN is Research Fellow of the China Project at the Council on Foreign Relations, New York; formerly a senior member of the Rand Corporation of California. He specialized in anthropology at Chicago University. He has travelled recently in the Far East and has contributed articles on China's foreign policy to *The China Quarterly* and other journals.

H. HOWSE is Assistant Head of the Far East Service of the British Broadcasting Corporation. He has spent many years in the Far East and he has broadcast in Chinese which he speaks fluently. He was Superintendent of Chinese Schools in Malaya until 1955.

R. HSIA is Senior Lecturer in Economics at the University of Hong Kong. He has been Visiting Lecturer at the London School of Economics, and also has been associated with Harvard University, Massachusetts Institute of Technology, and the Rand Corporation of California. He has published books and articles on varied subjects of the contemporary economic scene of China. He is at present engaged in a study on steel in Communist China.

C. T. HU is Professor at Columbia University, New York, Teachers' College. He spent a year recently at the University of Hong Kong.

G. F. HUDSON is a Fellow of St. Antony's College, Oxford, Director of its Centre for Far Eastern Studies and Advisory Editor of *The China Quarterly.*

He is a regular contributor to numerous journals on Chinese and world affairs, and he is the author of *Europe and China* as well as *The Far East in World Politics*.

E. S. KIRBY is Head of the Department of Economics and Political Science at the University of Hong Kong and the editor of *Contemporary China*. He is the author of *Introduction to the Economic History of China*.

W. KLATT, O.B.E., is Economic Adviser and a student of agrarian and economic affairs in Europe and Asia. He had been a consultant to United Nations agencies on several occasions. He has undertaken a number of surveys in various Asian countries in the course of which he has examined the possibility of applying the Soviet and Chinese patterns of economic and agricultural policies to developing countries.

J. R. LEVENSON is Professor of history at the University of California, Berkeley. He has recently spent a year at St. Antony's College, Oxford. He is the author of *Liang Ch'i-ch'ao and the Mind of Modern China* and also of *Confucian China and its Modern Fate*.

G. N. PATTERSON is a specialist on minority problems. He has spent many years in Tibet and on the Indo-Tibetan border. He was the founder some years ago of the International Committee for the Study of Group Rights. Among his publications are *Tibet in Revolt*, and *Peking versus Delhi*.

INDEX

SYMPOSIUM ON

Economic and Social Problems of the Far East

*Proceedings of a meeting held in September 1961
as part of the Golden Jubilee Congress of the
University of Hong Kong*

EDITED BY

EDWARD SZCZEPANIK

Senior Lecturer in Economics, University of Hong Kong

THE immense changes taking place in China and their impact on Asian countries pose problems of world importance. It was therefore fitting that the University of Hong Kong, founded in the year of the Chinese Revolution, should for its Golden Jubilee invite scholars from the universities of Asia, America, Australia and Europe to a symposium devoted to these problems.

The Session Chairmen were: Professor A. Doak Barnett (Columbia University), Dr Colin Clark (Oxford University), Professor Zelman Cowen (Melbourne University), Professor Morton H. Fried (Columbia University), Professor Marion J. Levy, Jr (Princeton University) and Professor Choh-ming Li (University of California, Berkeley). Professor E. Stuart Kirby (University of Hong Kong) was Chairman of the Symposium.

The papers, abstracts and summaries of discussions, published in this volume, are the joint effort of some eighty experts. They give a comprehensive view of modern China and her role in the Far East.

January 1963   **Hong Kong University Press**

Contents

III. POLITICAL CHANGES IN CHINA AND THEIR IMPACT ON THE FAR EAST

DAT

'73